A Sense of Place

RICHARD COBB

HOLMES & MEIER PUBLISHERS, INC.
IMPORT DIVISION
IUB Building
30 Irving Place, New York, N.Y. 10003

Cop. 1
Soc.

First published in 1975 by
Gerald Duckworth & Co. Ltd.
The Old Piano Factory
43 Gloucester Crescent, London NW1

© 1975 Richard Cobb

ISBN 0 7156 0877 0

Made and printed in Great Britain by
The Garden City Press Limited
Letchworth, Hertfordshire SG6 1JS

A SENSE OF PLACE

à

RAYMOND CLAVREUIL
Bourguignon de Paris
Libraire de la rue
Saint-André-des-Arts
mon ami depuis près de
quarante ans

Contents

Introduction

This book, which ranges from the geography of my childhood—
Tunbridge Wells, Sussex and Shrewsbury—to the border between the
French Empire and the Kingdom of Holland, north of Antwerp, and to
the central areas of Lyon in the early years of the Revolution, has as a
connecting link the theme of locality, an awareness of the relationship
between topography and history, and between place and the development
of a sense of the past.

The origins of the book's three sections are both varied and fortuitous.
The longest, which is also the last—that concerned with the *déclarations
de grossesse* made to a Lyon court during the first two years of the
Revolution—originated as a commentary on the possibility of using
this hitherto neglected type of documentation as a source for the study
of French social history in the late eighteenth century. I first used these
documents in the manner of an *explication de textes* for my graduate
seminar. I later wrote up the material, first as a paper for the Oxford
Past and Present History Society, and later in a longer version for a
communication that I delivered at the Anglo-French Historical Congress
held in Lyon in October 1974.

In this section, devoted to the misfortunes of Lyon female silkworkers,
to the simple skills and limited guile of the illiterate, I have endeavoured
to keep myself in the background, to avoid nudging my witnesses into
saying more than they wanted to say. Hence the considerable amount of
original documentation, the flavour of which I have tried to preserve,
even though the rough individuality of the girls has been filtered through
the formal, rather monotonous, medium of legal language, making each
brodeuse or *fileuse* or *fille de salle* express herself in a manner that she
would have been unlikely ever to have used in real life. The very
formality of the language may further conceal the fact that many of these
girls were certainly telling stories—*en train de raconter des histoires*—if
not outright lies, in any case a carefully doctored version of the various
and deliberately drawn out stages leading to their eventual seduction,
that would have presented them in the most advantageous light, as the
innocent and injured party. It would be necessary, for instance, to make
it appear that resistance had been prolonged when, in fact, it had been

feeble. It is reasonable to suppose, too, that some at least of the *déclarantes* may have been full-time or part-time prostitutes, more likely the latter, in a milieu and at a period when *le double emploi* was common with both sexes. The reliability of these girls as witnesses is in any case of no great concern to the social historian in search of the peripheral evidence that so often emerges almost accidentally from their accounts. The effect of a litany is thus unavoidable, and though this may not make for better readability, it certainly helps to emphasise the tragic urgency of the situation that faces each *déclarante*.

Apart from a brief incursion into the papers of the principal court of Lyon-Ville, for the past two years I have been working on the records of the French Ministry of Justice for the period of the Directory, the Consulate and the Empire, in the first place for Lyon, the Paris region, and the Norman Departments, and more recently for the north-east of France, and the Belgian Departments incorporated in the French Republic. Some of this material has been used in my *Paris and its Provinces*. It was while working on a supplementary box for one of the nine Belgian Departments, the Deux-Nèthes, of which Antwerp was the administrative and judicial centre, that I came upon *l'affaire Perken*. This case, though voluminous in documentation—it occupies an entire box—and though it spreads over the Franco-Dutch border in the early years of the Empire, contains, in its sordid simplicity, in its almost obsessive predictability, a sort of coherence that tells its own story, and that a very sad and desperate one. I decided, therefore, to treat it as a chapter on its own, without attempting to relate it to any more general theme, apart from those of time and place. Indeed, such is its finality, it would be almost impossible, as well as inartistic, to seek for it a wider relevance. If *l'affaire Perken* can indeed be witness for anything more than it actually describes, in great detail, and almost hour by hour, that can only be discovered in the telling.

The opening section of the book concerns my own development of a sense of the past. Although it is autobiographical I have once more tried to keep myself as much as possible in the background, in order to present an account of a middle-class childhood and adolescence in the context of place and period, in so far as both were likely to affect my own awareness at the time. For instance, the 'hammering' of my friend's father on the Stock Exchange must have represented the muffled echo of the slump of 1929–30 in the form that it reached a Sussex preparatory school. My sexual experiences at Shrewsbury might be taken to witness both for a period and for a class. Obviously, in my growing awareness of the national past, I was particularly lucky in my parents' choice of a school—for I lived within sight of one of the finest medieval and eighteenth century towns in England. And I also lived near a border.

Land frontiers will always have a particular appeal and excitement for the inhabitants of Great Britain. For quite a long period I would cross the frontier between France and Belgium at least once a week. The entry to the kingdom was epitomised by the rich cigar smell emanating from the *buffet de la gare* at Baisieux, as well as by the feeling of solid comfort contained in any Belgian café : potted plants, solid brasswork, *Le Soir*, an old-fashioned-looking newspaper attached to a wooden stick, as though Austrian influence had somehow lingered on after all these years. Whatever one's point of entry, whether at Baisieux, at Mouscron, or at Chimay, one would notice at once the change in domestic architecture, in the shape of roofs, in the colour of walls, in the quality too of the *pâtisseries*. *Le passage de la frontière*, even though repeated almost weekly, would thus appear as a perpetual *renouvellement*, though I suppose that the *frontalier* and the professional *passeur* must become immune to this subtle and agreeable sensation, must indeed end up by acclimatising himself completely to both sides of the frontier poles. One of the attractions of Belgium, however, at least to an Englishman, is that the frontier is never very far away, is accessible either on foot or by tram. I have walked from Belgium to the little fortified town of Rocroy; and I have taken the bus from Antwerp to Rosendaal. I have been down the Schelde estuary as far as the fort of Lillo, and have attempted to follow the old course of the Zwijn, a lost river, that disappeared some time in the fifteenth century, by the line of high church towers, on small hills, from Bruges and Damme to the neighbourhood of Ter Neuzen.

This awareness of place, of the imperatives of physical surroundings, is the theme which, I hope, gives the three parts of this book some sort of unity. As far as the order of the subjects was concerned, it seemed both logical and reassuring to begin with childhood and adolescence, proceed from there to death, and end up with at least the imminence of birth.

Some years ago, I gave a paper to a seminar in Princeton. My subject was dearth and hunger in France, my year was 1795. My host remained unimpressed by my account of great suffering, high mortality, and massive mobility, both from town to country, and the other way round. The poor, he observed, are always dying of hunger or disease, food riots always take the same form, the weather is often variable, winters are sometimes very cold, droughts are recurrent phenomena. So what? I did not really know what to reply. I think I assumed that the death from hunger even of a poor woman, two hundred years ago, was in itself important. When I first gave my talk on Perken at Shrewsbury School, some of the boys asked me, at the end, just what constituted the historical 'relevance' of a sordid, nasty little affair. I could only reply that it was something that had happened at a given place in a given period; and as the account of it, from start to finish, was remarkably complete, it appeared to me to be worth telling. I can imagine similar objections on the subject of pregnancy—after all, no very unusual phenomenon. I do not really know whether the pregnancy of an eighteenth-century Lyon *brodeuse* is historically 'relevant' or not. But a continued insistence on relevance would soon result in the abandonment of the study of the past and the end of history as we know it, that is as a cultural subject, enriching in itself. I myself am fascinated by the past, enjoy the actual process of research, and like writing what I believe to be a form of history, in the hope that others will enjoy reading it.

I am grateful to Mr Simon Schama, of Christ's College, Cambridge, for having, yet again, placed at my disposal his unique knowledge of Dutch history. For over twenty years, my work in Lyon has been made enjoyable and, I hope, fruitful, thanks to the unfailing kindness of M. René Lacour, Directeur des Archives du Rhône. My friend and former pupil, Viscount Morpeth, has given me valuable information and encouragement; and my friend and former pupil Tim Heald has constantly inspired me by his good humour, his *joie de vivre*, and his marvellous ability to express himself in writing. I would also like to thank Mr Lawrence Lequesne, senior history master at Shrewsbury, for having given me the opportunity to try out Perken on his pupils.

Worcester College, Oxford   RICHARD COBB
January 1975

PART I

Becoming a Historian

Becoming a Historian

'*Paasavamij lo jub*,' Arthur Cooper, a dark, mysterious-looking boy, asked me in a loud, distinct, rather pedantic voice, pronouncing *jub* like 'yoob'. I passed him the jam, or what was supposed to be jam, as our nearest neighbours looked up in surprise, though they should have been used to it. We had just finished the usual first course of yellowish-green lentils, with little black spots in them, and we were now on sliced bread and margarine, and home-made quince jam. We were sitting at three trestle tables, at each end of which were masters, matron, or Mrs Sir, the Headmaster's wife, who wore a bun, in the long dining room, decorated with faded photographs of the Acropolis, and of other Greek and Roman ruins—Sir, the Headmaster, had read Greats at Christ Church—and with the huge Frith print of the Coronation of Queen Victoria that I knew so well (I had even counted the number of heads to be seen in the Abbey, including the galleries—it came to two thousand, four hundred and thirty-three) for it hung on the wall over the Pig Table. This was a small table at the end of the room, with its back to the trestle and facing the wall. As I was the one boy then in the school who could make his milk come through his nose at will, an accomplishment of which I was naturally considerably proud, I had had plenty of time to study the serious Victorian faces present at that important occasion, which was the year of my grandfather's birth.

Arthur, whose brother was in the Foreign Office, and looked it, invented this language, based, I think, on some elementary gleanings of linguistics, presumably borrowed from his learned brother. Arthur, Nigel Farrell—who was from Tunbridge Wells like myself—and I were in the habit of using it in public, to exclude the other boys, and in private, as a sort of mental exercise and as a reminder of our apartness. Nigel and I were not nearly as proficient as Arthur in these exercises that were based on the interchangeability of consonants and vowels, as well as on inversions and the placing of the article at the end ('*heert u ootepfen?*' —this, at the dead of night, from Arthur's bed, next to mine, in the big dormitory). It was entirely Arthur's invention, though it was supposed to be the language spoken in the Empire of Khan, a large island with an elaborate principal and secondary railway network, several ports, and rich gold, diamond, and nitrate mines in the mountain range that ran from east to west, down the middle. The varying fortunes of Khan took up most of our spare time—on the playground, on walks, and on wet days, in the classroom. Arthur looked after the language, and was soon so proficient that we were scarcely able to follow what he was saying, though he had given us a careful grounding in Khanian grammar. It was my job to draw the maps of the island, and produce the imperial gazette. Nigel was in charge of diplomatic relations. Indeed, Khan was not entirely unrelated to what was happening in the world outside our school on the Beacon. I remember, for instance, Arthur lying down on one of the classroom benches, groaning horribly, and repeatedly pronouncing Last Words, in an elaborate and prolonged death scene—it lasted the whole of a Saturday afternoon—sinking very slowly, occasionally reviving. It was about the time that George V was recovering from a serious illness in Bognor (which as a result became Bognor Regis) and we had prayed for the King's health. After that, Khan became a republic, though there were numerous coups d'état, a military dictatorship, a naval régime, and, on Arthur's insistence, several revolutionary ones. When Arthur left the school, ahead of us, to go to Giggleswick, he carried on with Khan for the next three or four years, single-handed, presumably talking to himself. Nigel and I, left behind in Crowborough, had not the energy to continue with the story of our fantasy island and its intractable language in the absence of our taskmaster. Later, rather than go to University, Arthur went to Sweden and Iceland, learning both languages. Later still, he became something very important in Security.

After Arthur had gone, my energies were next directed, single-handed, towards the organisation of a pressure group that I called The Anti-Levitt League. Levitt was the head boy at the time, a bit of a bully, too, and he was believed, in the school, to be the son of a wholesale haberdasher from Brighton. His parents were rich, but it looked as though their wealth had been of recent origin, for they were visibly common. I did not need my mother, who always had an eye for this sort of thing and who very much approved of the exclusion of dentists from the Nevile Tennis Club in Tunbridge Wells (she was a doctor's daughter) to tell me that, because Mrs Levitt had dyed hair and wore a leopard-skin coat. Perhaps they paid extra fees for Levitt *fils*. Anyhow, Sir and Mrs Sir thought a lot of the Levitts. So I spent the whole of the Easter holidays organising the League, sending out circulars in inks in three colours to all the boys in my dormitory, urging them to take a stand against Levitt. Unfortunately, I missed the beginning of the following term owing to illness, and when I returned to school a fortnight late I discovered that my propaganda had misfired badly. I was told, even by

Nigel, that I had behaved like a rotter, and was put in Coventry. It took me a further three weeks, aided, it is true, by Levitt's own behaviour, to retrieve the situation. By mid-term, Levitt had acquired an unpopularity that my League could never have achieved for him. He had an accident, falling into a pit that some boys had dug for him—I had heard vaguely of the project from whispered conversations in the classroom, but had thought it best not to be in any way associated with it, as I was sure Sir and Mrs Sir would blame it on me. In the pit he was set upon by several large boys. Shortly after that, he was trapped into lying to the Headmaster, when the latter was doing his rounds and asked us all who had been talking in the dormitory. We had made sure of engaging Levitt in conversation. We all owned up, save Levitt, who had some sort of accent, and who, because we had got him angry, had been speaking loudly. The next day, we all made a delegation to the Headmaster's study. Sir thanked us for our honesty. Levitt was overthrown, and a nice boy called Dymott was appointed in his place. It was quite a *coup*, even more satisfactory than those of Khan. And I had learnt something about the advantages of the Oblique Approach.

This must have been more or less at the time of the Wall Street crash and the Slump. Sir announced, in mid-term, that a boy called Munro had suddenly had to leave. His father had been Hammered on the Stock Exchange. This sounded very painful. I missed Munro, too, for though he had never been admitted to the rites, language, and tumultuous history of Khan, he had invited me to his home in Hadlow during the previous holidays. I had cycled over there from Tunbridge Wells. His parents lived in a big house, in a park, within sight of the Tower, an eighteenth- or nineteenth-century Folly. His mother was French, and very beautiful, with a soft voice, and she had given us a delicious tea, with lots of little sandwiches and various kinds of scones and iced cakes, on a table consisting of several tiers of silver trays. She also seemed interested in what I was doing, asking me questions about my interests and making me feel wonderfully important. I wondered afterwards whether this beautiful lady had not been the cause of the Hammering.

We were walking in a long crocodile, two abreast, Nigel next to me, wearing dark blue raincoats, grey socks, and black shoes, dark blue caps with the letters B.S.C. on the front in red, across St John's Common, the bracken brown, and then along by the top of the golf course from which, on good days, one could get a view of the line of the South Downs. Leading us from behind was my favourite master, Mr Atkinson ('Please do not call me M. Ratkinson,' he would say. 'My name is Atkinson') whom we believed to be a bachelor, because he lived alone in a Country Club, hidden in rhododendrons, opposite *The Grange*, which was a rival prep school; later, much later, I discovered that he was divorced. As we came back down Beacon Road, we met, as we did several afternoons a week, an old man with a very red face and watery blue eyes, rather bent, whom M. Ratkinson had identified for us as Sir Arthur Conan Doyle. We used to hear a good deal more of that family, for, at night, when we were in the dormitory, his two sons, who had been at the school years earlier, were in the habit of roaring up and down Beacon Road in their racing cars.

On very fine days, from St John's Common, I could occasionally get a glimpse of the Wellington Hotel and the Mount Ephraim Hotel in Tunbridge Wells. It was both reassuring and disheartening to live thus in exile, but in sight of home. When, for one reason or another, I was very depressed—for instance, when Nigel was not speaking to me as a result of the collapse of The Anti-Levitt League—the two hotels, the one white, the other red, represented beacons of hope. My sentence would not last for ever. Not that I was often that unhappy.

We stood in line, in the classroom, with our French primers open in our hands, faced by the Green Pig, a master called Mr Wright, who was very small, had tiny whitish bristles instead of hair, and always wore a green plus-four suit. The French primer revealed a life totally different from the violent up-and-down history of Khan. It was one of marvellous stability. There was *Monsieur*, bearded, of course, and wearing a morning-coat, striped trousers and spats, and there was *Madame*, cuffed, collared, corseted, encased, moving about as if on casters. There was Ernestine, or Célestine, or Emmeline, the parlour maid, in black, with white smock and cap. There was the blonde Micheline, an Alsatian or a Bretonne, perhaps a relative of Bécassine—but I did not know about Bécassine then—who was the kitchen maid, and rather stupid. She could not read, and tended to get *Madame*'s orders wrong. But she was good-natured and generous, and the children knew that there would be titbits set aside for them in her ample kitchen. There were two children, Jean and Lucie, both dressed all the time in sailor suits, Jean with a red pom-pom on his round cap, Lucie with a long blue ribbon flowing from hers. They were either at school—a *lycée*—or, on Thursdays, were taken to a park, with trees lined up like soldiers, green tubs of orange trees and an elaborate, metallic bandstand—there was always a band playing—and generally they bought balloons. There were also scenes at well-decorated tables, the napkins laid out fan-shaped. There were *anniversaires* that were not birthdays, and they put out their shoes in the grate on the eve of *Noël*. On 14 July, prize-giving : they also won most of the prizes, being exemplary children, always doing what they were told, always polite to their parents, always considerate to the maids. Immediately afterwards, 15 July, *les grandes vacances,* departure for les Sables-d'Olonne. Later, when I was seventeen, and first went to Paris, I was not in the least surprised to discover that the family I was staying with always spent the summer in a villa that they owned in les Sables-d'Olonne. It had been in my French primer. All this seemed quite timeless, like the sailor suits, the hoops, the bandstand and the band, though I suppose my French Family must in fact have been of pre-1914 vintage. At the time, I put the sailor suits, the hoops, and the clothes, which were the sort I would see in back numbers of *Punch*, down to the fact that these people were French, and so could not be expected to dress like ourselves. Later, when we left the Green Pig for Mr Ingram, a tall, sad-looking man wearing rimless glasses, we were promoted to Tartarin and to the drawings of Caran d'Ache, both of which I enjoyed very much. It was quite a surprise suddenly to discover that French, like Greek, which I was doing with Sir, and unlike Latin, could be both fun, and funny. Mr Ingram was the only married member of staff, apart from Sir. With the social mobility that seems to charac- terise the profession of prep school master, he later emigrated to Oxford, running a Health Food store near The Queen's College. I used to go and see him, looking as lugubrious as ever, when I went up to Merton. He seemed satisfied with my progress in French irregular verbs and with my familiarity with the *subjonctif passé*.

Most of my relations, however, did not have much time for the French. My mother was something of an exception in this respect. When she was eighteen, she had been sent to Paris for a year, at the time of the Dreyfus Affair, staying with a family called Chéron, and she had nearly died of pneumonia, as a result of having to attend, in mid-January, the *bains publics* in the rue Racine. The Chérons, who lived nearby, in the rue de Cluny, and who were apparently quite well-off—they gave brilliant dinner parties at which there was always much patriotic talk about the honour of the French Army—did not have a bathroom. *Monsieur*, conventionally, did have a mistress, *une femme entretenue; Madame,* while the maid was doing her piled-up hair in the morning, used to tell my mother that all men were beasts. My mother was easily convinced of this, and retained the belief, for the rest of her very long life, that French males were immoral and selfish, and that French females were appallingly oppressed. Why did they stand for it? Madame Chéron did not even have full control of the housekeeping expenses. And yet she seemed utterly resigned to her domestic slavery. It was perhaps not an unduly distorted impression of the Parisian middle-class family in the lush years of the Third Republic; and, indeed just the better to conform to type, the Chérons had no children. The other thing that my mother retained of the Paris of 1900 was that French doctors were unbeatable, a prejudice I have always shared with her. She had been nursed back to health, from the threshold of death, by one of the bearded, frock-coated variety.

My father, on the other hand, belonged to that generation of franco-phobes, so numerous in the middle classes of the inter-war years, and no doubt even more numerous in the Sudan—Fashoda remained very much on my father's mind as an example of French perfidy—who were liable to come out with such well-worn myths as that which stated that the French authorities had been so mean, during the First World War, as to oblige each British soldier, taken from a base camp in Calais, Etaples, Boulogne, or le Havre, to pay for his railway ticket to the Front. My uncle, a surgeon-commander in the Navy, was in the habit of stating that the French were immoral as well as dirty and unreliable, that they all suffered from unspeakable diseases, that the Germans were reliable and our blood brothers, and that it had been a tragedy that we should have been at war with them, and that this must never happen again.

Fortunately, to redress the balance, there was my Aunt Emily, the matron of the Eye and Ear Hospital at Tunbridge Wells, who had gone into nursing because *her* Great Aunt Emily had done so at the instigation of Miss Nightingale (she had later suitably died of yellow fever, while matron of a hospital in Buenos Aires). My aunt had nursed in a French military hospital in the Great War, and was a convinced franco-phil, regularly following M. Stéphan's French lessons on the wireless, and taking in a magazine called *La France*, which was published by the *Alliance française* and had as an alternating cover *la Semeuse* and a cockerel. She went each winter to Menton, returning with sprigs of mimosa. One of my moments of true glory at the Beacon School was at the daily distribution of mail, when I was handed a postcard from Paris, of the *bouquinistes*, one of them wearing a bowler hat and a sort of cloak, with a wintry Notre-Dame in the background, in sepia. This was an ace, to be displayed with pride. For, in our colonial past of the late '20s and early '30s, letters from Nigeria, the Gold Coast, India, the Sudan —I even had difficulties in doing swaps with my huge supplies of Camel Corps pinks, greens, and mauves—were commonplace, so many prep school boys having parents there—their photographs, in silver frames, would be on chairs beside their beds, in the dormitory: whereas Europe was very rare indeed, especially once Munro had gone, after his father's Hammering.

There were also two of my aunt's friends, Miss Kent and Miss Davies —Tunbridge Wells in the '20s and '30s specialised in such combinations —Miss Kent tall and graceful, who dressed like Queen Mary, and had reddish hair, Miss Davies, small, gnarled, and rather satanic (it was Miss Kent, I believe, who had the money) who lived in a pretty house with a front step in coloured tiles, just off Mount Sion, and who three times a year withdrew to Paris, staying always in the same first-floor suite, Hôtel Victoria, facing on to the gilded statue of Joan of Arc, place des Pyramides. They, too, were enthusiastic gallophils.

At my school, thanks to M. Ratkinson, history had become my favourite subject by the time I was twelve. It helped to satisfy my enormous curiosity, both about the past, and about foreigners and foreign countries. My awareness of the past had been early instilled in me by my grandfather, who had the tremendous merit, in my eyes, of having been born in 1837. But my father, too, after his return to England, had, perhaps unwittingly, contributed to my insistent curiosity in this respect —I upset him very much when I was about seventeen by telling him that I found the Duke of Newcastle much more interesting than Stanley Baldwin. For my father, who before going to South Africa as an officer in the Royal Engineers had been a civil engineer in Peterborough, was both churchy, and had a ready line in black-and-white. I had begun to accompany him, first of all in the beloved flat lands of the Stour and the Colne estuaries, on his expeditions to the great Essex and Suffolk churches. We had been together to the little church of Copford, in the shadow of the eighteenth-century manor house : and he had shown me the piece of the skin of a blasphemous Dane, kept under glass, and presented to the church by an eighteenth-century Cobb parishioner; and he had visited the graves of my Cobb forebears, clustered together in a corner of the churchyard, the earliest dating from the seventeenth century. I do not know what they had all done, perhaps they had been labourers, or farmers; but, for a hundred and fifty years, they seemed scarcely to have moved out of the village; and my grandfather and great-uncles had only moved the six miles into Colchester. Later, I went with my father on tours of Kent and Sussex churches, and, very soon, got into the habit of going off on such trips on my own. In my holidays, by the time I was fourteen, I had taken in and sketched most of the parish churches of the Tunbridge Wells area and had prospected windmills at Mayfield and Goudhurst, ruins at Bayham and Scotney Castle and Ightam, castles, Roman roads, abandoned canals, disused railway lines, old mill ponds and forges.

While still going to day school in Tunbridge Wells, and every day during the holidays, after I had been sent as a boarder to Crowborough, I had been in the habit of stopping off, for an hour or two, in the late afternoon, and sometimes for half a day, at Major Moreland's chaotic antique and junk shop, on Mount Pleasant, near the central station. I would come down the steep hill, catch sight of myself in the window of a photographer's shop—and it was a sight I did not like, my eyes seemed to be popping out, my fair hair would not brush down, sticking up in tufts on the back of my head—but the Major, if that was what he had been, for he had spent a great deal of time in Spain and South America, did not seem to find anything unusual about my appearance, and left me entirely alone—I had my own corner—while I read through back numbers of the *Illustrated London News*, or scrabbled in trays full of old coins. The Major often let me take away a handful or so of these, and was generous with gifts of pretty Tsarist stamps, in delicate pinks and whites. I used to listen to the Major's cronies. My mother never worried about my long absences, knowing I was either at More-land's, or looking through the old prints of Kentish and Sussex localities in Hall's bookshop in Chapel Place. I liked the Major, because he treated me as an adult, told me about the places that he had visited, and left me alone when I was engrossed in his collections of old magazines and illustrateds. During the school holidays I also spent a great deal of time with a bed-ridden Danish lady—at least, my parents *said* that she was Danish, though I now think that she was probably German, which was still considered a bad thing to be in the '20s—Miss Pohlman, who was looked after by a companion. She had tremendous prestige in my eyes, because she came from the other side of the Great Divide, having travelled extensively in Northern Europe, including Tsarist Russia, before 1914. As I sat on a low chair beside her bed, in the overcrowded room, both bedroom and drawing room, I could feel close to that lost, and so longed-for, world, as seen through her eyes, and recollected through her accounts of childhood.

Mrs Martin, who started coming as my mother's daily when I was nine, and who stayed with us for over thirty years, had started life on a farm in Horsmonden. I once met her father, a bearded, patriarchal figure who ran an oast house near Brenchley. As she was the eighth or ninth child, she had gone into service as a scullery maid, in a big seaside hotel at Folkestone, when she was thirteen. She had then been in service in a succession of families in Folkestone, Canterbury, Eastbourne, and Tunbridge Wells, coming to us from a local doctor's, who had three daughters. Clearly, from what she told me, there was little that she can have missed of *la chronique scandaleuse* of a middle-class professional family, as observed either from the kitchen, or from the marvellous observatory provided by the early morning breakfast tray. As a school-boy, I did not fully understand all her allusions: 'Miss Nathalie, she was a proper one, she was' or 'Miss Meta, she was a real imp, always up to something', and I could not guess quite what that would be, though Mrs Martin seemed to equate sin with high spirits and a feeling of independence. She certainly seemed to have known what had been going on in the doctor's house, as well as in the garage, and what she had not directly observed she had been told about by one or other of the girls, both of whom had confided in her, wishing, I suppose, to have an unbiased and even admiring witness of their various exploits with male members of the Tunbridge Wells *jeunesse dorée*, the Old Barn Set. I was far more puzzled by the rather wheedling, whining deference of Miss Ralph and her 'sister' (she was in fact, I learnt much later, her illegitimate daughter) when my mother went to them for a fitting, in a stuffy, evil-smelling room, full of tailors' dummies, at the unfashionable end of the town, behind the old Town Hall. Social historians have lost incomparable witnesses of the chronicle of middle-class family *mores* with the disappearance of the domestic servant. Nothing can ever quite replace the impudent stare from the World Below Stairs. And there often existed too a sort of complicity between the children of the house and the servant. Mrs Martin certainly knew a great deal about the doctor's daughters that their mother neither knew nor would have dreamt of.

Growing up so soon after the war, I had become rather sick of the exploits of the *Boy's Own* hero 'Baby-Face' Carruthers and his sort, who were always getting the better of some villainous-looking Germans, stealing the plans of the secret battle 'plane, sabotaging the zeppelin at its moorings, or capturing single-handed the latest model of a U-boat, while the crew looked on startled. Carruthers always had everything his own way, it was a walk-over. My dislike for him was further stimulated by the fact that, in such stories, the coward, the traitor, the Englishman who let the side down, was generally called 'Cobb'. All right, I would be a 'Cobb' too. I felt that the Germans could not have been all that bad, all that inept, or all that beastly; and I desperately wanted them to win, at least once in a while, it was only fair. And, as I suppose all boarders are more or less consciously a little bit homosexual, I used to idealise the mysterious German boys of my own age (they were growing up under Weimar), imagining what it would be like to get to know them.

But the Germans were never my Favourite Foreigners. While at the Beacon, I chose, as a form prize, Motley's *The Rise of the Dutch Republic*; and, for several years, the Dutch enjoyed pride of place in my personal pantheon. They seemed to possess all the desirable virtues. They were Protestant and blond—and I had learnt from *Westward Ho!* that Spaniards, and anyone else totally reprehensible, were always dark, even very dark—they were brave and honest, they loved freedom; at my age, they were already engaged in holding back the flood waters of the threatened dike with their little fingers; their oppressors were dark, fanatical, and cruel. Egmont and Horne were unsullied heroes; I had a portrait of William the Silent in my bedroom at home, and, like the little children in the streets, I wept when I got to Breda. Motley certainly set me on my way. I communed with the Sea Beggars, applauded each Dutch victory, admired Dutch steadfastness, shuddered at the barbaric cruelty of Alva, was repelled by the scheming trickery of Granvelle

—and what could one expect of a Cardinal?—and regarded Philip II as evil incarnate. It was good black-and-white stuff. It was the function of history to illustrate the triumph of the Protestant Cause.

Of course, my own observations did not entirely correspond to such a simplistic view of history, race, and nationality. There was a boy at my school called Hook, who, on Sundays, would go off alone to the little Catholic church with a tin roof on Crowborough Green. He was a nice, quiet, gentle boy, and I liked him. Also, he seemed quite normal; physically there was nothing that distinguished him from any of us, and as we were in the habit, in the evenings, of standing on our beds, and displaying our penises, for comparative shape, length, girth, it was evident that he was like nearly all the rest of us—for foreskins were out of fashion with middle-class doctors in the '20s, along with tonsils, adenoids, and appendix—though there was one boy who had retained his, and showed us how he could roll it over; anyhow, he was a special case, his father was in Nigeria, and this must have had something to do with it. Hook was perfectly fair, not at all like one of Alva's soldiers. But he went off to church before having any breakfast—not that he was missing anything very much, just soggy porridge, bread and margarine— so that, once, he fainted, and we were not surprised, it was the sort of thing that happened to anyone out of line. And I noticed, at the end of one term, that his father had a beard, which rather gave the game away. There was no doubt about it : Hook was different. He had to be, for, in both my schools, I had suffered from the thoughtlessness of my parents in inflicting on me the initials R.C. It was all very well being Richard Charles, but I had had more than enough of always being called Roman Catholic Cobb.

Hook was the only boy out of step. All the rest of us were Anglicans, not so much out of choice, as because it was something that one simply fell into or inherited. Our religiosity was very much what the French would describe as *églisier*; and it corresponded to the sort of attitude I would later experience in the Army, when signing up 'Luckies' (recruits). Name and Date of Birth, Place of Birth, Religious Denomination? 'What's that, mate?' 'What *religion* are you?' 'What do most of the lads say?' 'C of E.' 'Put me down C of E then.' Some of the boys said their prayers, one or two rather ostentatiously. My own connection with the C of E involved me in a particularly shaming experience. We had been asked to tea by the vicar's wife, and were sitting in a large anteroom with black-and-white tiling on the floor, eating currant cake. I was suddenly taken with a pressing need; but could not pluck up the courage to ask our hostess where the lavatory was (I did not know what to *call* it, for, at home, my mother had imposed the non-committal translation from the Afrikaans, *Het Zeckere Plaats* : 'The Certain Place').

I was soon contemplating with horror a trickle of yellowish water, that soon became a gush, running down my leg, forming a wider and wider pool on the tiles. I tried to cover up the dreadful evidence of my disgrace with my foot, but it was to no avail. I was detected, taken away, had my shorts removed and put out to dry. I was wearing my best tweed suit, reserved for party occasions, a lightish-brown outfit. I could never abide the suit again, and have never since worn brown. It seemed the colour of disgrace and detection. Of course my parents were informed of my insult to the Established Church.

Thus I grew up in an enclosed, class-bound, introverted, enervating, very English world, in a definable geographical area that social historians may some day describe as the Great South-Eastern Preparatory School Quadrilateral. I know, though I did not know it then, that prep schools existed in other places—Captain Grimes had even been employed somewhere in North Wales. But certainly, in the '20s and '30s, the *hauts-lieux* were to be found mainly in a rectangle of territory stretching from the coastal bulge of East Kent, more or less to the level of Southampton Water, and, inland, up to the level of Guildford, Otford, and Maidstone. They were thickest on the ground on the Channel Coast: medical opinion in the time of Horder and Dawson of Pen favouring the damp sea fogs as a remedy for all the usual boys' ills. All those who have written novels and short stories about the miseries of prep school life have nearly always placed their chronicles of petty woes in Bexhill or Seaford. These seem to have been the areas of maximum concentration, with armies of crocodiles, clad in a variety of hues—blue and red, mauve, chocolate and gold, green and yellow, in stripes, diagonals, lozenges, zebras, heraldic effects—marching up and down crossing one another on the promenade, or on the way to or from the public swimming bath, exchanging looks of hostility and pity, possibly even abuse, many-hued throngs, the colour changing with the rapid turnover of bankrupted or runaway headmasters. But even Crowborough was well to the centre of this massive masturbation reserve. There were two prep schools in the place itself: the Beacon, and, just down the road, hidden in a thick, confused jungle of rhododendrons, pines, and cedars, the Grange. We seldom met. Walks must have been parcelled out as a result of some sort of territorial treaty, leaving us the Golf Links and St John's Common, and the Grange the border of Ashdown Forest and the lower village, down to the level of the railway station, so that we very rarely ever saw the boys from there, in their light-grey blazers tipped with a creamy stripe (a colour which gave rise to very obvious jokes on our part as to its origin). We never played matches against the Grange, and only went there once a year in the summer, on one of those utterly agonising occasions designed especially to torture already sorely tried and underfed little middle-class English boys in the '20s and '30s, to sit through a Shakespeare play, put on in the unkempt garden of the school, by some amateur performers : all that awful ranting and shouting, all that heavy fooling, all that diarrhoea of confused words ! What was most retained from these dreadful sorties was the peculiar, fuggy, *niffy* smell of the boys' changing-room—it was generally believed by ourselves that the denizens of the Grange never wore underclothes—as well as the annual, or possibly bi-annual, succession of headmasters, as they followed one another, presumably into bankruptcy, dishonour, disgrace, or with the petty cash, or with the current matron, or with both. Though the headmasters came and went, they, too, appeared to wear a sort of uniform : mustard-coloured plus-four suits, a brown hat, and a stick, possibly to distingish themselves from Sir, similarly attired, winter and summer, in hardy oatmeal, with thick brown woollen stockings.

There were three more prep schools between us and Tunbridge Wells, two of them, unlike the Grange, 'recognised', and so visited for matches. Each had a distinctive, unfamiliar, and therefore unpleasant smell. We also had matches with a huge establishment in Uckfield, the inland capital of prep school-land, the inmates of which wore rose-pink caps. Tunbridge Wells itself possessed two—one of them, that I had previously attended, Rose Hill, was not considered by my mother to have 'a very good class of boy'; indeed some of my companions there had had parents in trade. It was run, rather chaotically, by a retired naval officer and by his French mistress, who had a moustache, wore a *camée* (I believe representing Marie-Antoinette) and whom, for some reason, we called 'Gus'; the naval slant was emphasised dramatically by the presence in the garden of a full-size merchant ship, the funnels of which could be seen, red, with black bands, above the trees, from Mount Ephraim, at the top of the Common, adding to the illusion that Tunbridge Wells was a seaside town and that Mount Ephraim, which, in those days, was the parade ground for scores of wicker bathchairs drawn by little ponies, was in fact on the Front. The other, Eversley—chocolate brown and beige—collapsed, in the usual manner : headmaster plus matron plus cash, while I was at Crowborough. We went as far afield as Brenchley, Mayfield, Tonbridge, Rotherfield, and Goudhurst. But we had no direct contact with the coastal hordes.

No English institution could have been more evanescent than the English preparatory school of the inter-war years. Anyone could start one, absolutely anyone could finish one. The supply of boys, like the extraordinary naïveté and trust of parents, many of them, of course, absent on imperial duties, was limitless. Yet such is the binding strength of collective loyalties, even in institutions so shadowy, that each one developed its own group personality, so that wherever we went on our unwilling visits to our 'recognised' neighbours, we felt that we were indeed penetrating into the tribal lands, observing our companions, much the same size, with much the same skin-colouring, speaking much the same language (though, not, of course, Khan) as ourselves, to try to pick out the external signs of depravity and abnormality. It was not just that they *smelt* differently. They seemed totally alien. A boy who went to a succession of prep schools, as some of my richer companions were in the habit of doing, would presumably acquire a succession of totally different personalities.

Of course, even then, I had peeped over the walls of the Quadrilateral. I knew the flatlands of the Essex-Suffolk border : for this was my grand-parents' country. I had often stayed with my naval uncle at Southsea, walking over, at low tide, to Hayling Island, then a wild place full of larks, sea birds, and lonely stretches of dune and sand. I had explored many of the churches of North Berkshire, where my favourite uncle drove around as a country doctor. He was a tremendous gossip, and endlessly inquisitive about people, indeed, I think he only practised medicine in order to get into other people's houses; I would sit waiting in his car while he did his rounds, and, after each visit, he would come back to the car triumphantly with some new item of malice, rather like a researcher after a good day in the Archives Nationales. I had even been far north (and its northness was unequivocal, as it was indicated in its place name) to Northampton, where my father's godfather, a Welsh-man of very High Anglican leanings—there were choirboys in mauve, which I had always taken as a very romish colour—was the vicar in an affluent parish. Even so, it was a narrow, class-bound geography, the catchment area of the *Morning Post* and the *Westminster Gazette* (I never even heard of the *Manchester Guardian* before going to University), a very English area, too, but of the southern variety. My mother typified many current prejudices in this respect : the Irish were lazy, mendacious, dirty, improvident; they lived like animals, near the goods station, and went to the Catholic church, which was at the wrong end of the town. The Welsh were dishonest. Had I not noticed too how *swarthy* Dr Davies was ? The Scots, on the other hand, were all right, I think because my mother had known a great many of them in the Sudan, where, at one time, Sir James Currie had been my father's chief. Any other evidence as to the existence of the 'lower classes' was provided by the hordes of domestics : those, starched and collared, who opened the front door when I went with my mother to visit her friends, those who brought in the tea, those who drove the older doctors in their carriages, the two uniformed chauffeurs in bottle green who sat in the front of 'Frisky Fanny's' magnificent green-and-gold electric car, bolt upright, so that it was impossible to see which one was actually driving, while Fanny, a former Lady-in-Waiting to Queen Alexandra, closed away behind a glass panel, and dressed in old rose, graciously waved to the roadmen as she went on her stately and silent progresses down Major York's Road; the armies too of nannies who would come and fetch us from the agonising dancing lessons in the ballroom of the Spa Hotel, occasions rendered all the more disturbing by the presence of the imbecile son of Austen Chamberlain, a little boy whose tongue hung out, so that he constantly dribbled; my own nanny Kate, brought from Essex—she later married a man called Love, who had a handcart and whom my mother was convinced must be of gipsy origin, he was so dark, and they moved into a slum behind the *Kent & Sussex Courier*; and the whiningly deferential Miss Ralph and her 'sister', the alarming inhabitants of High Brooms, fortunately at a safe distance from the Royal Borough.

But what we lost in the extent of our English geography, we fully made up in terms of local mobility. We were always on the point of moving, moving or just completing a move. I can vaguely remember two or three addresses in Cumberland Gardens and Cumberland Walk, several more in various roads that lead off Grove Hill. At one time we were living in a pretty wooden cottage in Kentish billboard, which was actually on the Common, near the Pantiles, at another, we were somewhere up near the Girls' High School. For some weeks we lived in a house that had a green turret, at the top of Madeira Park—Baroness Olga, the Royal Borough's only White Russian, lived a few doors down. I can remember that house, because it had a hexagonal addition to each room connected to the tower, and because I used to sit in the Tower looking at back numbers of the *Illustrated London News*—I liked best the drawings of half-naked savages—which went with the furniture. Indeed, most of these places were let furnished. And what furniture! I often think my parents must actually have enjoyed moving, because there cannot have been much saving in thus constantly criss-crossing through the town, our own possessions piled on a handcart. According to my sister, seven years older than myself, we did sixteen moves when I was between four and nine; and she could recall a further seven addresses in Frinton, from my birth to when I was four. I believe some of these moves must have been in some way related to my father's intermittent, irregular spells of leave from the Sudan. But even after he had retired, they continued. On the whole, I rather enjoyed them, because in this manner I was able to see the inside of a very wide range of houses; and, all my life, it has been an almost obsessive urge with me to get my foot in the door, to get behind the façade, to get inside. That, after all, is what being, or becoming, a historian is most about—this desire to read other peoples' letters, to breach privacy, to penetrate into the inner room.

It might sound heartless—I did not feel heartless at the time—but, when we were waiting to embark for Normandy, we spent much of our time, in a camp near the London Docks, helping the fire brigade and the ARP to dig people out of little brick houses that had been destroyed by the blast of V-Ones; it was horrific enough, yet here was a scatter of letters and postcards all over a backgarden, there the intimacies of a girl's drawer draped in the trees. One felt pity, certainly, but also a great deal of curiosity. And in Germany I made the most of my powers of search, not so much to look for stolen cigarettes and food, as to get into people's houses. On the whole, then, I enjoyed the moves. Curiously, when I was nine, we moved into what was supposed to be a temporary resting place, like all the others, and we stayed there for about forty years. I have no idea what produced this breach with habit on the part of my parents.

I owed, then, much to my school at Crowborough, to M. Ratkinson, to Major Moreland and his shop, to all the old people I knew as a child in Tunbridge Wells—not just Miss Pohlman, but also old ladies with parrots living in Nevile Park—to my grandparents, to my Cousin Daisy, who, in her filthy bedroom, in my grandfather's house, also lived entirely in the past, amidst years and years of back numbers of the *Daily Mail*. Poor Daisy was retarded, and, at forty, was still as much as at six a devotee of Teddy Tail; when my mother actually succeeded in getting into Daisy's room, and in getting Daisy undressed and into the bath, for the first time in about twenty-five years, she had to clear away fifteen years' worth of *Daily Mails*. There was little else in the room.

But, by the time I left for Shrewsbury, I probably owed as much in this respect to *places* as to *people*, and above all to Tunbridge Wells itself, a town in which I was aware of every possible itinerary, in which I found safety, security, a marvellous continuity, still so compelling that, even now, after being away from the place for well over ten years, I can still, in half-sleep, experience the reassurance of its so familiar geography : the approach to Chapel Place, the two large eyes, an optician's sign, by the steps at the end of Cumberland Walk, the gentle curve of Calverley Park; the always-to-be-remembered view of Mount Ephraim, and the bowling green in Birdcage Walk, from the large bow window, leading on to a wrought-iron balcony, of my mother's drawing room; the climb up Grove Hill, the stone crocodiles at the entrance to Camden Park, the stone swan outside Swan Cottage, in Little Mount Sion. I was proud of the house facing on to the Common, for a long time the headquarters of the local branch of the Conservative Party—as though the Conservative Party even *needed* a branch in such a place— in which Thackeray had written *The Newcomes*; proud of the fact that, from the age of nine, I was living in one of a sweep of Regency houses, curving towards Birdcage Walk, with its two stone arches at each end, and that, in our house, Sarah Grand had written most of her novels. I was of course very proud of the Pantiles, of the old shop with wooden boarding, of the well, and the little eighteenth-century balcony, over a cobbler's shop, from which orchestras had played. I was proud of the Salerooms which had once been the Great Sussex Hotel, and of the big solid house on Mount Sion, next door to Miss Kent and Miss Davies, in which Queen Victoria had lived as a girl. I was proud of the church of King Charles the Martyr, once a chapel-of-ease, through which ran the county boundary between Kent and Sussex, and which contained some fine seventeenth-century plaster moulding and was topped by a pretty white wooden clock-tower which looked very Dutch. I was proud of Burton's splendid Calverley Crescent and Calverley Hotel, of the fine Regency houses facing on to the Common, of the eighteenth-century shop in which one could buy Romary's water-biscuits, the town's only industry. I was even proud of the early-Victorian gothic of Holy Trinity. I delighted in my mother's drawing room, its window, with the curtains drawn at night like a stage set, a room into which even the horrors of war somehow failed to penetrate. I felt that all this past belonged in some way to me, that I was benefiting from it, and I greatly enjoyed showing it off to my school friends. I have often thought how dreadful it must be to live in a completely new country, or in a new town; each time I have been to the United States, I have felt a strong sense of deprivation, as if something that was as necessary to me as the air I breathed was lacking. There was that awful sameness, the visibly contrived past, as much in the Howard Johnson motels, invariable in their furnishing, as in the uniforms of their remarkably surly personnel, from one ocean to the other. I believe that much of the basic unhappiness of that society can be attributed to this relative lack of a past, to this cultural indigence. For deserts are not enriching, and it is only the human past, the vestiges of human achievements, that can give us a sense of identity and pride, and above all, the feeling of time and period. I never have regretted the fact that, like most people of my generation, I was taught history in the old-fashioned way, that is in terms of kings and queens; and this is not because I ever thought individual kings or queens particularly important —though some were undoubtedly fun, and I very quickly acquired a marked preference for the Hanoverians—but because the simplest way of measuring time and of identifying a period, at least in our own national history (which should always be our first concern) is in relation to different reigns. 'Queen Anne' or 'the Regency' is immediately identifiable in physical terms, 'Georgian' represents a whole world of reassurance, extreme sophistication, elegance, and beauty. Henry VI could somehow witness for the strange twilight world of the fifteenth century. We are fortunate in thus possessing a national time scale immediately understandable to any English child. To reject it, in favour of some meaningless continental or world system of measurement, would be to turn our backs on our own national past. It would be a form of impoverishment and amputation just like knocking down an old building, to make way for a car park or a bus-station.

The prospect of Shrewsbury was very alarming, when it was first proposed to me. For one thing, there was no personal or family reason why I should go there: Gresham's or Felsted would have been more natural. What alarmed me most was the fact that the place was so far *north*, much farther north than I had ever been before, and that it was so near Wales. But, from the moment I first got out at the elaborate neo-Gothic railway station, built over the Severn, I recognised in the town both an ally, an escape, and an endless delight as a treasure of visible history. Shrewsbury in the '30s was probably one of the most perfect medieval towns in England. It was still largely fortified, and one could do an almost complete circle on the walls overlooking the great bend in the Severn that had dictated the town's origin. Frankwell, Butcher's Row, Wyle Cop, the precincts of St Julian's, and St Alkmund's, the black-and-white houses in a little street leading to the town end of the Kingsland Bridge, offered a varied mass of fifteenth-century domestic architecture. There are few finer churches than that of St Mary's, attended by generations of Salopians. The contemplation of the great Jesse east window, in fifteenth-century Flemish glass, with its vivid blues and greens, offered an immediate and much-used consolation for the philistinism of my house. And I have always enjoyed the naïve poem relating the dramatic fall of poor Cadman, a Salopian Icarus, who, in the early eighteenth century, had sought to span the 'Sabrine stream' in human flight.[1] There was the old town mint, down an alley-way; and just outside the walls stood the abbey church, in pink Shropshire sandstone like St Mary's, St Alkmund's, St Julian's and the ruins of old St

---

[1] The poem is recorded on a tablet placed on the west face of the tower of St Mary's, below the spire. The original eighteenth-century tablet has disappeared; and the present stone is a fairly recent copy. I owe this information to the kindness of Mr Stacy Colman. The poem reads:

> 'Let this small Monument record the name
> Of CADMAN and to future times proclaim
> How by'n attempt to fly from this high spire
> Across the Sabrine Stream he did acquire
> His fatal end. 'Twas not for lack of skill
> Or courage to perform the task he fell:
> No, no, a faulty cord being drawn too tight
> Hurried his Soul on high to take her flight
> Which bid the Body here beneath good Night.
> Febry 2nd. 1739 aged 28.'

Chad's. A few miles north of the town, a large mound indicated the site of the battlefield, also marked by the Battlefield Church, a fifteenth-century building in perpendicular, isolated in the middle of a field. But best of all were the Georgian splendours of Belmont, especially the magnificent Swan Hill House, flanked by proud stone lions with curling tails and surmounted by an elaborate coat of arms.

One of the many strokes of good luck that came my way, almost as soon as I went to the school—and one certainly needed a little good luck, when plunged into that brutal society—was the presence on Kingsland of an art master, Mr Woodroffe, a Birmingham man with a Birmingham accent, who, though teaching at the Schools, was somehow not really part of them, being able to look at that excessively inbred community with the rather amused detachment of the outsider. Mr Woodroffe thought that both the masters and the boys were fearful snobs—as indeed they were—and he really came to life in the town. He was a leading light in the local art club, and, thanks to his protection, and to my own preoccupation with pen-and-ink, when I was sixteen I too became a member of the club. This represented a double bonus; for I thus had a pretext to 'go down town', to 'cross the river', so pressing, so impecc-able, that even my utterly barbaric Housemaster could scarcely object to it, though he clearly considered that so many contacts with the locals in some way endangered my moral integrity (if he had bothered to make himself even a little aware of what was going on in his own House, under his very nose, just beyond the uncrossable frontier of the green baize door separating the boys from the Housemaster and his family, he would have realised that the threat to my innocence—such as it was —did not come from the other side of the Severn, but up in Kingsland itself). Secondly, my bi-weekly visits to the art club gave me a sense of detachment from the obsessive atmosphere of the House, as well as adult friends, of both sexes, who seemed to be genuinely interested in my sketches and who were prepared to treat me on my own merits, as an individual, and not as a boy who wore a blue jacket, a straw hat with a chocolate and gold band, and a white collar.

In other words, the Shrewsbury Art Club offered me something that I have sought ever since, and have, happily, always succeeded in finding, even when, or especially when, in the Army : an escape from collectivity, a place of my own, an assertion of my own individuality, a minimum of privacy. No one who has not spent a number of years as a boarder in institutions—preparatory school, public school—can understand the immense sense of relief to be gained by the action of turning a key in the door, of shutting oneself in, or rather, everyone else out. In my House at Shrewsbury, I could only be alone in one of the upstairs lavatories, and then but for a couple of hours in the evening. The days

• •

were spent, either in classrooms, or in a study, with four or five others, their desks in close proximity, the contents of the desks known to all, the nights, in bedrooms in which there were from six to twelve beds.

The Art Club did not offer me the immense gift of a room of my own —I had to wait for the holidays for that, and for much of the rest of my life I would derive a great sense of peace from the security of a hotel room or a *chambre meublée,* and I have been in vast numbers of both —but, through it, I gained access to private houses, and some of the members, sensing my longing for a little privacy, were in the habit of lending me their keys in the daytime. Eventually, I had three or four more or less permanent bases, in the relative anonymity of the old town (where there was always the danger of being seen by a master or an prae-postor) or, better still, in the more proletarian, safer areas down by the Welsh Bridge. If my Housemaster had known of my secret, he would no doubt have suspected the worst. All I did, in fact, in the hide-outs, in these 'rooms over the sweetshop', was to enjoy the unusual and blissful experience of being alone.

Mr Woodroffe and the Art Club served me in another important way. My sketching-pad was the most convincing of passports for the outward journey. Working for Mrs Hardy's Drawing Prize, I could go to Buildwas, Stokesay, Acton Burnell, Church Pulverbatch, Bishop's Castle, to a score of ruins, fortified churches, castles, and villages on the Welsh Border, beautiful, faraway, quiet places, right in the Housman country. I was, of course, extremely pleased when I won the Prize, but the greatest pleasure had been getting away from Kingsland, and from all those noisy, inquisitive, interfering boys. Even a system so scientifically repressive, so carefully calculated to stifle individuality and distinctiveness as an English public school of the '30s will have its unsuspected loop-holes; and the discovery, and subsequent exploitation, of one of these greatly adds to the enjoyment of escape. It is like a blow, albeit a tiny one, struck against the whole system, the brutal monolithism of imposed assumptions and accepted opinions.

I was not long in discovering another of these loopholes, one that was trebly satisfying, in personal terms : Shrewsbury prided itself on its tradition of cross-country running, and the School Hunt was said to have been one of the oldest athletic clubs in England. There is plenty of evidence that it was already in existence, using its somewhat weird formulae (by which boys, all of them in fact two-legged and similarly equipped, were divided into human beings—huntsman, whips, gentle-men of the runs—and animals—hounds) and running over farmland, marsh and bog, in the 1790s. As some of the runs were obligatory for the whole school, I was not long in finding out, rather to my surprise, that I was better at long-distance running than the average, and, indeed, that the greater the distance, the better I would do. And some of the runs averaged from ten to twelve miles. I can still recall most of them, with evocative names like the Bog, the Redhill, the Longden, the Newton, the Cruckton, the Bomere Pool, the Long, the New, and the chaotic rabble of the Tucks, like an army in disorderly flight, a run on which the whole school participated. Most of the runs took us in a general south-westerly direction, towards Pontesbury, Church Pulverbatch, and Leebotwood, which generally meant, in Shropshire conditions, running against the wind on the outward journey, and having the wind behind one on the homeward run. I do not think this had been calculated to console us at the prospect of the return. More simply, it was because Kingsland was situated to the south-west of Shrewsbury, so that this general direction was the easiest point of exit and re-entry. But there was one run, the Bomere, that ran due south, towards Condover, another that headed due west, past the big Lunatic Asylum (Shropshire is a great place for Lunatics) towards Bicton Common; a third, known as the Long, started at a point beyond Atcham, at a great sweeping bend of the Severn, about eight miles to the east of Shrewsbury. This was particu-larly heavy going, as, once one had crossed the river at Atcham bridge, one pounded along a long, hard, straight road, ending at Sir George Hill's Column, seen from afar, at the south-eastern exit from the town. This was the only run that did not actually start from the school gates. I think it must have dated back to the time when the school was still in the town, in the old building, now a museum and the town library, both guarded by a statue of Darwin.

I cannot remember in detail all the different itineraries; what most stays in my mind is the sense of exhilaration and escape, at the outset, when one was running with one's back to Kingsland, battling against the south-westerly winds, along the cinder path, heading for the cemetery and the railway that ran through Meole Brace. A running vest and shorts were the very symbols of freedom, releasing me, for a time, from the elaborate visible hierarchy of vestimentary rank—this or that sort of collar, dark or coloured socks, jacket open or closed over waistcoat (an English public school boy of the '30s was particularly well equipped to understand, later in life, the outward manifestation of rank, speciality, and privilege, in a country like eighteenth-century France), and reducing me to the far more anonymous ranks of a much more extensive collect-ivity. It has always seemed to me that, if one were considering escape from a place of confinement, the best possible equipment, as well as the most effective means of not attracting attention, would be the simple clothing of a cross-country runner. No doubt it has been done many times.

Away, away you ran, Kingsland farther and farther behind, with a steady stride, geared to regular breathing, towards the wonderful freedom of the open country, over boggy fields, cutting directly through a marsh, getting your legs scratched by the brambles and thick undergrowth of the woods above the black, sinister, deep Bomere Pool, past semi-ruined brick kilns, past the tall water-tower, past the Wiches, cutting diagonally across the fields of Dayhouse Farm, past Newton Farm, over the wet, muddy Pulley Common, Allfield Farm, across Rea brook, up Sharpstones Hill, over the styles into Juice Tank Field, on to Hanwood or Horton. The runs were always in winter, generally between October and December; and I can still remember a dead tree, stark on the horizon, like a hangman's tree, silhouetted at the top of the hill, against a leaden sky, somewhere on the way to Hanwood—it was one of my *points de repère*. At this time of the year there would be any amount of the comforting red Shropshire mud, the mark, on your returning, panting and sweaty, right up your shins and the back of the running pants, half way up the back, of one of these brief incursions into complete freedom. You noticed the sky, and the pitching roll of the country, as it bore you along, crashing, long-strided, towards a brook or a reddish bog, pulling up hill, as you always had to on the return journey, for Kingsland is high up, or with the ground all at once giving way under your feet, as you ran at twilight through a small wood, the branches brushing your face. You passed right through the marvellously dirty Shropshire farmyards, occasionally pursued by an alarming Welsh sheep-dog; you caught sudden glimpses, as it grew and grew in height, on a rise in the land, of a church spire or of one of the squat fortified towers of the border country; you caught distant, moving perspectives of great Georgian country houses—Namier's Shropshire gentry had clearly done well for themselves—and, in a woodland clearing, down a vista, might appear a Tudor manor house, in black and white, or a moated ruin. The animals you could scarcely notice—you ran too fast and too noisily. You ran under low railway bridges, and along parallel with the lines to Hanwood or Church Stretton; sometimes, with a side glance, you would see the merrily-moving line—cream and brown—of a train; and sometimes the passengers would wave to the lonely panting runner. You passed institutions : asylums, hospitals, isolation hospitals, old people's homes, pumping stations, and sewage farms, brickworks, slag-heaps—for much of this, within running distance of Shrewsbury, was vintage Industrial Revolution country—country pubs, council estates—but your breathing made too much noise for you to hear what the children were shouting, probably nothing very amiable, if they recognised in the runner an escapee from Kingsland—small goodsyards, sawmills, water towers; you ran through country churchyards and struggled over potato fields. There was endless variety and wealth, a constant sense of discovery, the excitement of shooting off, at an angle like a runaway tram, of running through reeds that came up to your chest, of hacking your own way through copses, as if you were an explorer, or an advance scout of an invading army, in a rough, hostile land : and hostile it was, this Mary Webb country : and superstitious. And, on good days, on the outward journey, you could take your bearings on the gentle, bluish undulations of the Stretton Hills, of the Long Mynd and the craggy sinister Stiper-stones, on the steep arched back, like a porcupine's, of Pontesbury Hill, or on the distant Breiddens, all so inviting, and the Breiddens with an even more compelling and mysterious message, hinting at Wales, a foreign land, just over a couple of valleys—and you could hear Welsh in Shrews-bury itself on Thursday market-days—the biblical land that could be seen, rising and falling, in lines of blue and tawny hills, from the school playing fields, a reminder that freedom lay to the west.

The runner sees mostly forwards, as the countryside jogs up and down; the farther he runs, the worse his vision, so that the final pull up Hospital Hill, towards the Moss Gates and Kingsland, would be made when one was almost blinded, and, in a race, one could just distinguish the blurred white faces of lines of boys, blue lower down in their jackets. If you ran into the middle of the two lines, as into a paddock and with no one ahead, it meant that you had won, and this was a brief moment of glory, of supreme satisfaction, for one also ran to win. And, sometimes winning ('killing' was the word, and it would have been more appropriate to your own condition, rather than to the win) you acquired, in the strict hierarchy of a boy-imposed tyranny, a sort of inviolability, some-thing in itself very desirable. The greatest satisfaction was the sense of escape, the knowledge, too, that if things got really intolerable, you could thus take to the open country, without money, and with no bag-gage, and head either to Wales, or southwards, to the Clun Forest and the Black Mountains, though exactly what you would do on arrival was uncertain. It was perhaps not the mere chance of speedy legs and stamina that made of my friends Clover and Edward, the Irish boy, as enthusiastic runners as myself. At one time, we had a plan to run through the night, in an effort to reach a friendly vicarage somewhere deep in South Shropshire; and Edward did in fact run through the night, reaching Church Stretton in the early hours, and wretchedly reporting, hungry and penniless, at the police station. He was brought back, wet, miserable, and covered in a blanket, in the Housemaster's car.

Three or four years ago, I was killing time on a Sunday morning, in Paris, walking in a misty Luxembourg, between the long lines of rather ghostly trees. There hung over the gardens the relaxed stillness of the Parisian Sunday; the bells of Saint-Sulpice were clanging lazily for eleven o'clock mass, and small family groups, heavily wrapped up, were to be seen, walking towards the exits, holding packages tied up with gold thread and containing *pâtisseries*. All at once, emerging from the murk of the rue Claude-Bernard, on the other side of the boulevard, there came a white, bearded figure, running gracefully and powerfully, crossing the street without a break, and heading diagonally straight across the gardens, disappearing, as if he had been eaten up by the fog, down one of the central avenues. It was a beautiful sight, the emblem of independence, of individuality. I wondered who the firm young runner was: perhaps a student from *Agro*, farther up the street. It did not much matter. Here too was a lone flier, someone who looked ahead, as he ran, busy with his own thoughts, and as free as the air. I was reminded of my time at Shrewsbury, and of my early days in Paris, when, in order to continue running, I had joined *le Stade français,* using their changing rooms before setting out for long, misty runs in the wintry Bois de Boulogne, returning, tired and refreshed, by *Métro* (Vincennes-Neuilly). And there is more in running than all I have described. The runner acquires a sense of speed and of distance, he can feel the wind, the contour of the land, the terrible bumpiness of cobbles, he can experience even more fully, because more dramatically, the gradual transition from city, via *faubourg,* to the open country: the last green bus, the lowering of the heights of houses, low-lying cafés and restaurants in the *faubourgs,* the immensely long grey wall of a factory, spelling out DEFENSE D'AFFICHER over half a kilometre, a bridge swinging towards one, straightening itself out, the tops of trees, as seen by the runner, as they too jog along, when he raises his head, tree-tops unseen by the walker. New visions, and new angles, on a very ancient scene; and the enormously comforting sense of having earned one's journey's end. It may seem a long way round to what is my principal theme; but I do indeed believe that the visual impact of running is useful to the historian, particularly to the historian mainly concerned with people on the move, on foot or on their toes, as most people would be, in the eighteenth century, if they wanted to go anywhere. Nothing can offer more dramatically the liberating sense of the open road, as it unrolls before one, seen over the tops of a series of hills, with its endless promise, if not of success, at least of change, of the hazards of encounters with travelling companions, of the companionship of the traveller on foot. Forward Whittington. *Et en avant la musique.*

Perhaps I have run too far and too fast. Now it is necessary to return from the cool air, from the rolling fields, and the red earth, to the stuffy smell of boys' socks, of football boots, the confined, intolerant, cruel smell of the changing room of No. 1 the Schools. At least I would come back covered with the honourable *stigmata* of the red mud, my visible

passport to a grudging respectability within the collectivity, more plod-
ding, less mobile, more conformist than myself. I might be wearing my
house colours on my running vest; but at least I was running for myself,
and not for my brutal and strictly anti-intellectual House.

This, too, like my prep school, was a narrow class-bound community.
But the range of both class and provincial origin was much wider than
it had been at the Beacon, recruited mainly from the south-east, or from
children from the south-east whose parents were serving in Africa or
India. In my first bedroom, a long room with a view on to the Wrekin,
its tawny, striped back making it look like a huge, science-fiction-sized
mole (but the sight of the Wrekin was also a promise of freedom), the
Londoners and the southerners were in a minority; and, owing to the
almost fawning predilection of our reptilian Housemaster for Liverpool
'top brass', there was a large, brutal, bullying contingent of the sons of
wealthy Unitarian families from the north-west. These, in my first two
years in the House, monopolised, and abused, most of the positions of
power in the House. Under this régime, new boys ('new scum') were
subjected to a gamut of physical and moral humiliations—having football boots thrown at one in the changing room, being tipped off a table
after being made to sing to the assembled House in the dining room,
being beaten for having failed in the Colour Exam (what are the House
colours of Tombling's? Maroon and French grey—and so on) while the
conversation at night of the northerners was principally concerned with
the expensive makes of cars owned by their parents, who, on Speech Day,
might be seen arriving in Rollses and Bentleys, the wives with dyed hair
and leopard-skin coats : in fact, north-western Levitts. Any suggestion of
intellectual interests was ruthlessly branded as something sinning against
the prevalent orthodox philistinism; it was not even a muscular
philistinism, for these big louts, so good at beating, were not particularly
proficient at any other sport, and there was only one School colourman
among them. What they *were* good at was making life hell for small
boys, shouting *Doul* (the local word for 'fag') as though anything that
was not an immediate, breathless response, as ten small boys came
careering up the stone passage, would be met with an instant beating,
showering favours and 'T' notes (*billets doux*) on the boys they loved,
and organising elaborate, collective beatings. The Liverpudlians were
much the worst, and it was with genuine amazement that, much later
in life, when I was a soldier stationed at different times in various places
in the north-west, I discovered that Lancashire people were the most
generous, warm-hearted, open, and amusing folk I had ever come across
in England. These, it is true, were not Unitarians, nor 'top brass', but
ordinary working-class people, hospitable and kind.

At Shrewsbury, I became very conscious of being from the south-east, tending to huddle together, defensively, with the Londoners and with those from the Home Counties, most of them sons of professional people, one or two of academics (including the son of Professor Collingwood, one of the unhappiest boys in the House). One of my closest friends came from the old Cambridge family of Clover. His father was a clergyman, and the boy played the school organ at services : an occupation that the Liverpudlians apparently found immensely hilarious ('Jo on his organ again', and that sort of thing). Clover had to go away for a year, as the result of a nervous breakdown. Subsequently, he was beaten by the Headmaster, for having written for every answer in the Certificate 'A' examination 'Dig a latrine' (Question : 'You are about to order your platoon over the top. What do you tell your men?' Answer : 'Dig a latrine', and so on). Later he won an organ scholarship to Emmanuel College, became a music-teacher in a South-African public school, where, he wrote to me, the boys were even *more* philistine than in No. 1 the Schools, and was eventually shot dead while trying to escape from an Italian prisoner of war camp in North Africa. I remember hearing, with amazed envy, of the presence in the school of a boy whose father worked on the *New Statesman,* and who did not have to join the Officers Training Corps, as his parents disapproved of military service (mine thought it would do me the world of good); but of course he was in School House. Later, on the History Side, I met the son of a Balliol tutor, Kenneth Bell; but he, too, was in another House. My own was not at all typical of the school as a whole, either in content, or in mental (if that is the right word for brutishness) attitudes. There were, for instance, a number of Welsh boys scattered throughout the school, most of them the sons of Cardigan and Merionethshire solicitors—a very useful contact, as I was to discover when, as a Lecturer at the University College of Wales, I found it necessary to send solicitors' letters to a succession of my landladies who, because I gave sherry parties to my students, accused me of immorality. And there was also a strong Dublin Protestant connection, as well as a contingent of Ulster Protestants. Brian Inglis, whose parents lived in Swords, for instance, was to be one of my contemporaries on the History Side. Another, Arthur Pyper, had a wonderful fund of stories about life in Northern Ireland. From friends made in class, outside the House, it soon became apparent that there were plenty of corners of Enlightment on Kingsland. Unfortunately, I was not in one of them.

It would be impossible to describe an English public school in the '30s without some reference both to masturbation and to relationships between boys. Perhaps, later in this century, there will be historical textbooks on the '20s and '30s, studies of the education of the professional classes,

with such titles as 'The Masturbationary Decades'. For I very much
doubt if anyone could describe the '60s and '70s as masturbationary.
Perhaps there might be something in the Whig view of history. Certainly,
in my experience, one of the great illusions of nineteenth- and twentieth-
century schoolmasters and educationalists was that sport discouraged
boys from masturbating, exhausting their energies on the river, on the
football field, in the swimming baths, or at Eton fives. This was a complete fallacy. Sport, on the contrary, was a positive stimulus to masturbation. In the course of the three or four years that I spent in my House,
I was able to reconstruct, mostly from the tell-tale noise of heavy breathing and the increasing precipitation of the creaking of beds, the weekly
calendar of this activity—or, more politely, the Salopian Masturbator's
Fasti—and *Fasti* they were, for, as it turned out, they coincided, with
amazing accuracy, the sort of accuracy that would bring joy to the
quantitative historian, with the official *Fasti* of the term's big sporting
events. Not only that, the calendar was *inter*-sport. For instance, after
the Bomere Pool, or one of the other big runs, *all* the beds in a bedroom,
or most of them, would be creaking away like anything, as if the race
were being re-run, at a very different tempo, not just those of the
runners, who might legitimately feel that they had fully earned this
simple, inexpensive reward, but those, too, of footballers, rowers, swim-
mers, Fives champions, cricketers, as well as of those who took no interest
in sport, unless one was to regard masturbation itself as one. It would
be the same after a House or School soccer match, though a win would
always produce more noise, heavier breathing, more precipitation, than
a lose.

It was as if sports were out to compliment one another in this vigorous
and noisy manner of acclaim. Indeed, the phenomenon had some of the
aspects of a primitive religion, of tribal rites and fertility cults (even if,
as we were so often warned in those days, what we were doing was likely
to render us in later life *in*fertile). It was the one thing that might bring
a normally quarrelsome, contentious bedroom momentarily together, in
an agreeable awareness of general guilt and of shared complicity. It was
a secret that we had together, and that secret would go with us later to
the classroom, to the sixth-form library, to the chapel, to the essay class
held in one of the master's houses, the memory of which would give one
the impression of belonging to a sort of underground society. However
much we might dislike one another individually, we shared the memory
of these rites, and could look forward to a predictable succession of
similar ritual celebrations in the future. I think this was the one effective
way in which 'the House spirit', something that was considered so desirable by Housemasters, did in fact express itself.

Predictably, Friday and Saturday nights were the big masturbation

nights. Morning masturbation was very rare, possibly out of a sense
of decency, more likely because we had to get up so terribly early. The
older boys would stand by the showers, in their pyjamas, watching the
younger boys run down, naked, often with erections, straight from their
beds. But the Friday and Saturday sessions were never openly collective;
there was no exposure; each masturbator ploughed his solitary furrow,
at least going through the pretence of not hearing the others, though it
was only a pretence. Certainly, the semi-clandestine nature of the
operation added to its general excitement. There was never in my House
—or at least in my bedroom—any sort of open *bacchanale*, the boys
standing naked on their beds, such as apparently went on in a neigh-
bouring House run by a clergyman, reports of which percolated through
to us as the result of a sudden mass expulsion of monitors, one of whom
was expelled in a manner reminiscent, for its qualities of high drama, of
the methods employed by the mad Tsar Paul. He was batting for the
Schools, in the First Eleven, in a match against Repton. A messenger
was seen to go up to him, there was a brief whispered conversation, and
they walked off the pitch together. The boy was given just the time to
change out of his cricket things, and was driven down to the station by
the reverend. It was just like Paul, in the film *Alexander Suvorov*,
screaming at the Ismailsky Regiment, when they turned up on parade in
their old, Russian uniforms: 'Left turn, by column of fours, to Siberia,
MARCH.'

I have referred to the tribal aspects of these rites. But each House
undoubtedly represented a distinctive tribe; and the essence of tribalism
is diversity, secrecy, and hostility to other tribes. What might be good for
us, as Salopian Ibos, might not be at all to the taste of the Salopian
Yorubas of School House. I can only speak for my own tribe; and though
I had some very good friends in other Houses, both on the History Side,
and later, at Merton, there always remained a curious reticence in this
important matter. I imagine that the calendar must have been much
the same throughout the school. But that was all. There may even have
been Houses containing only a minority of masturbators, though I doubt
it.

So much for masturbation, in the relative, very relative, intimacy of
the House bedroom. There were, too, of course, relationships that were
much more intimate. While pretty well every boy masturbated, more or
less regularly, certainly at least twice a week, a few—and I think that
they *were* a few—would couple up. When I became a bedroom monitor, I
was vaguely aware, as I fell into deep schoolboy sleep, of the furtive
movements and the giggles that, at regular intervals, would come from
a bed on the other side of the room, diagonally across from mine, the
occupant of which could certainly have been described as *généreux de sa*

personne, a well-built, tall, fair boy, with a very good complexion, well-shaped eyes and rather long lashes, and prepared, so far as I could judge —though I never attempted the experience myself—to get into the bed of any boy in the room. After my regular evening sessions in the lavatory, reading Namier, in preparation for Oxford Entrance, I would bang away with my slippers as loudly as possible, as I made my way down the long corridor to my bedroom, so as to warn the boys of my impending arrival; and I would often hear the noise of pattering feet, as the tall fourteen-year-old, or whoever had enjoyed his favours, returned to his bed. In the morning, I would sometimes note, with interest, that the tall boy's pyjama bottoms covered the bottom of another boy, whose own bottoms hid the rather elegant *rondeurs* of the posterior of the hospitable night traveller. I am glad to say that I never detected in this boy the least embarrassment at the revelation of his particular choice of the night before, though the favoured one might blush scarlet.

There were mysterious allusions, from the Great Outside, for we were not a very keen rowing House, to what happened, or might happen, Up River. This was when two boys took out toothpicks, very long skiffs, or an ordinary rowing boat, from the Boat House, and headed, on a Saturday or Sunday afternoon, upstream, beyond the Welsh Bridge. One gathered that there existed Up River idyllic bathing places, concealed among the tall reeds, or drying places in the long grass on the bank, semi-tropical *nids d'amour* to suit the Savage Heart. One of the House-masters was in the habit of giving the new boys illustrated talks, in his study, one by one, on the Dangers of Going Up River, showing them photographs of nude boys standing up in the shallow water, or their bodies mottled by the shadows of leaves in the summer sun, that he had taken, from a vantage point in a tree that he regularly occupied, such was his devotion to the repression of Vice. They must be very careful to resist invitations to Go Up River; or, if they did, they must come and tell their Housemaster exactly what happened. I never myself went Up River; the only time I ever took out a toothpick, it capsized, when one of my oars went in deep, and I had to swim to the bank, my feet still in the straps, dragging the toothpick behind me. No more Up River for me after that.

Religion, too, at least of the Low Church variety that was officially favoured, quite unwittingly witnessed the development of relationships, some of them entirely harmless, a few of them certainly harmful. The chapel, especially at Sunday evensong, with the advantage of candle-light, and when the boys were at their cleanest and pinkest, brushed, their faces radiating an engaging reverence, was a sort of *bourse d'amour.* Roger Peyrefitte, in *Les Amitiés particulières,* has brilliantly described the stimulus afforded by a certain kind of collective religious fervour, in a closed, inbred community of adolescent boys, to the development of extremely passionate and even lasting relationships, both between *collégiens,* and between boys and individual masters. He was writing about a Jesuit *internat* in the south-west of France; but, differences in the service, and the use of the confessional, apart, it might have been written about Shrewsbury in the '30s. I think, too, that many of my contemporaries were much more aware than most people of some of the homosexual undertones of Hitlerism, especially of the collective fervour of the Hitlerjügend. I was still at Shrewsbury at the time of the Night of the Long Knives, in June 1934 : the circumstances of Roehme's murder were not lost on us. We knew about that sort of thing. Perhaps those German boys, in their leather shorts, masturbated, collectively or individually, all for their Führer.

Thus sport, religion, and even literature conspired to kindle the flames of passion, love, and lust. For Shrewsbury, in the '20s and '30s, had already produced an abundant and explicit literature on the subject of homosexual relationships : novels with such revealing titles as *The Bending of the Twig,* written by Old Salopians, who had, as it were, remained in the Kingsland groove, sometimes long after they had left the place, idealising, with the benefit of nostalgia, that Garden of Love, gave a sort of literary respectability to what was in any case natural enough. Housman's *Shropshire Lad,* read throughout the school, added an agreeably doom-ridden dimension to the very understandable lust of boys cooped together, dressing and undressing together, able to map out in detail, and to memorise, underneath the uniformity of clothing, one another's corporeal geography : freckles on the shoulder, a birth mark on the left buttock, the line of an appendix operation—like a rowing-boat, an eight, at the side of the lower abdomen—the dimension of the penis, the perfection or imperfection of the bottom, the shape of legs, the elegance of a neck, the delicacy of a shoulder, the colour of skin— pink and white was the fashion, though there existed a minority of depraved connoisseurs who were already aware of the smoky allurement of *la peau mate*—the size, shape, and colour of eyes, the proneness to blush, the infinite variants of the glance : innocent, pseudo-innocent, mocking, provocative, brazen, inviting, tender. In short, the exploration of the whole vast territory of an adolescent, masculine *carte du tendre,* a dangerous geography.

Add to all this the fact that, with the English class system perpetuated, as it still is, from one generation to the next, creating its own, often incomparable, biological specimens, public school boys tend to be unusually good-looking, even endearing in their wilting fragility. Salopians are not perhaps *en masse* as handsome as Etonians, their looks enhanced by the black-and-white effects of their clothing, but they still rank very high in terms of physical appearance.

Finally, in the '30s, girls were not even to be seen, for miles around. The few female employees on Kingsland were without exception hideous; in my House, the maids had huge patches of sweat under their armpits. The girls from the Grammar School were supposed, too, to be common. A few hardy souls, one of them a Persian boy, another a Dutchman (Oh dear! not at all what I would have expected from a compatriot of William the Silent) would come back with stories of girls who were to be had, *moyennant finances*, though the Persian boasted that he got them for nothing, in the neighbourhood of Copthorne, where the KSLI had their barracks. And George Rudé was to tell me, years later, when we met in Paris, that he and a couple of other monitors from his House, —the one the Housemaster of which warned the new boys about Up River—had regular access to a town girl, on Wednesdays and Saturdays, in the boiler-room of the House. The girl was in fact the boilerman's daughter, brought twice a week across the Sabrine Stream for this purpose. It tickled me to think of George thus engaged in the cellar, while the Housemaster revealed, in his study, to some new boy, the Dangers of Up River. It was rather like *What the Butler Saw*, in a jerky old film on a seaside pier.

The House, then, was pretty awful, though bearable, at least by me, and I can bear a good deal. I am inclined to think that it was in fact even worse, though no doubt he would not agree—and it is difficult to draw up an accurate comparative scale of awfulness—than Severn Hill, under 'Cuddy' Mitford, as described, *dans une prose justement vengeresse*, by the Welsh artist Kyffin Williams, in his recent autobiography.[1] Kyffin and I were contemporaries, but, being in different Houses, I do not think that we ever met, though I heard of his talents through the art master, Mr Woodroffe, who thought very highly of his paintings. I was, however, very friendly with two boys from his House, both of them on the History Side, David Gieve, and Richard Wainwright. Mitford was an insensitive, unimaginative, sports-mad brute; but my Housemaster was probably worse and certainly less excusable. For fear of being thought an intellectual—and he was certainly a fine scholar, and a very effective teacher of the classics—he gave the Lancashire louts a completely free hand. Happily, their reign did not last all my time in the House; the supply of Unitarians must have temporarily dried up. Kitchin the rowing coach, and Housemaster of Ridgemount, was also a brute, of a particularly nasty kind; he delighted in imitating boys with unusual accents. Ian Hogg, a friend of mine, who was a Glaswegian, and an

[1] *Across the Straits*, London, 1973.

extremely shy boy, was constantly pounced upon by Kitchin to speak in front of the form. Tombling, too, was a sombre tyrant.

Fortunately, apart from the House, there was the school, and it was a very good one. In my first year, I was taught Greek by the Headmaster himself, Canon Sawyer; and it was a memorable experience, greatly adding to the enjoyment in that language that I had already begun to feel at my preparatory school.

All the time that I was at Shrewsbury, I had English masters who were inspiring and enthralling, and this tradition has been happily maintained by the presence of that incomparable spell-binder, MacEachran, 'Kek', who, unfortunately, came to the school a year after I left, but whom, fortunately, I at once got to know and appreciate. The first English master that I had was not only enthralling, but wildly eccentric as well, even by the difficult standards set by the profession. His name was Captain Banks; he had had some sort of naval career, interrupted, so the Salopian chronicle would have it—and schoolboys are notorious myth-makers—with some brutality: a court-martial, after he had flooded a score of localities on the Clyde estuary, by driving the destroyer that he commanded too fast and too close inshore, while drunk on the bridge. There was certainly no doubt about his drunkenness. He was a huge, moon-faced, hilarious six-footer, with red hair and an even redder complexion. We went to him for First Period, before break-fast, when he was at his most fragile. This generally took place in artificial light; and it was our habit, before he came in and sat at his desk, to set all the lights swinging, so as to give the impression that the whole room was moving in a gentle ground-swell. It was an operation that was constantly and demonstrably effective. The Captain would take a line on the ceiling, holding on to both sides of his desk, while beads of sweat began to appear on his forehead. He would turn gradually from his usual reddish-mauve to a sickly, livid whitish-green: it was only a matter of time—ten minutes, a quarter of an hour—during which, from our various corners, we kept up the regular swinging, before, a ghastly green, he rushed off the dais and made for the door, returning after a few minutes, his eyes still watering, but firmer, his breath fortified with Scotch. We sometimes improved on the swinging by attaching threads of cotton to his form note-book, with the class list, which one of us would then pull very gently, once the Captain had sat down, so that the list would move very slowly before his eyes. He was, in fact, a humane and very amusing master; more surprisingly, he had a very real feeling for the mighty cadences of Milton—and, being so close to Ludlow, we were all well schooled in that great poet, the whole school attending the ter-centenary performance of *Comus* at the Castle—and even succeeded in communicating this sense of Miltonian rhythm to someone as tone-deaf as myself. Despite his alarming build and incandescent appearance, he was a kindly, gentle man. He was also, I think, a very lonely one. Something had gone awry a bit earlier in his career—a broken engagement, or something of that sort—and he had taken to the bottle. Things got worse after I had left the school, and, eventually, he had to leave. During the War, Captain Banks was discovered by the Headmaster living in a seaman's home in Devon. Thanks to subscriptions from masters and former pupils, he was moved to the more comfortable quarters of a private nursing-home, where he died of *delirium tremens*.

Later, I was taught by the great S. S. Sopwith, who, after a long career at Shrewsbury, started a second one at King's School, Canterbury, where he lived until his death in 1974. Many Salopians owe their appreciation and understanding of Eliot, Auden and other modern poets to this incomparable, sensitive, and eloquent teacher of English. I can still hear 'the Swith' reading to us passages from *The Waste Land,* the evocation of 'dull October days', and 'the smell of smoke in passage ways' that, totally unpoetical though I am, have remained in my memory as startling images of ambience. If history has always remained for me very much the depiction of place, of ambience, as well as of narrative, and if it has always appeared to me as inseparable from literature, this awareness—and it may be one of my principal faults as a historian, for I believe that history is a creative art, and not a mere exercise in research, scholarship and measured judgment—is entirely due to the inspiring teaching of Mr Sopwith. How would I, without the guidance of this master of rhythm, sound, and evocation of place and season, ever have discovered, on my own, the old gravy smell, the cabbagey smell, of the basements of Bloomsbury boarding-houses kept by declining ladies, the stale smell of genteel loneliness, the paper napkins, pink and yellow, the tiny chunks of grapefruit, the minuscule portions of fried-bread and bacon of the breakfast table of inter-war London years, the hurried, half-ashamed 'Good mornings', before the lodgers—unattached, mousy ladies, sad-looking clerks, lonely people of uncertain professions—hastily hid themselves behind their morning papers, each bearing his or her name; the underground Torrington Square world, washed away by the blitz, my favourite retreat from the institutional life of an Oxford College, my regular plunges into the joys of anonymity, of being unattached and unknown, freedom spelt out in potted plants, antimacassars, dark, bad oil paintings, huge, forbidding mahogany dressers; how would I have come to appreciate the sad, seedy poetry of such loneliness, evoked too by Anthony Powell, and by my Merton contemporary, Angus Wilson, in their descriptions of the yellow stucco South Kensington scene, had I not been guided in the beauty of words by my English master in the Classical Fifth and the History Remove? Mr Sopwith was not only a spell-binder; he was also an understanding and enlightened Housemaster. His House was one of the happiest in the school.

French, at Shrewsbury, was treated, at least by Mr Brooke, with a suitably gallic levity. It was a matter of leavening a very little teaching with a great deal of clowning. Mr Brooke regulated the administration of this enjoyable mixture with a device of his own invention : a battery-operated miniature traffic signal attached to the side of his desk—green : you may laugh (at one of Mr Brooke's schoolboy jokes, of the vintage : Christmas in a German lunatic asylum—'God Bless ye jerry mentalmen' and suchlike), amber : prepare to stop laughing; red : stop laughing, and resume Racine. The natural pomposity of Racine and Corneille could not possibly stand up to such treatment. Mr Brooke was much more than an *amuseur public*, for *le Grand Roi, le Grand Siècle*, its stuffed formalism, its ordered drill, were crying out for such joyfully irreverent treatment. Our French master was in fact quite discerning, for, when dealing with Molière, the stop-go signal would be put aside, and he allowed Molière himself to give the cue for laughter. It is a pity that Mr Brooke was never let loose on the collected speeches and ponderous prose of General de Gaulle. The signal would have been a most useful commentary on the President's more solemn statements.

We were fortunate, then, in our English masters, and in the exuberant fooling of Mr Brooke, who, behind this tremendously funny façade, did in fact conceal—succeeded in concealing from all those who did not know him very well—a simple, natural goodness, and a wonderful, utterly innocent piety. In later life, he became a clergyman, ending it as an enormously effective and well-loved vicar of a country parish in North Essex, as well as, most improbably to those who knew him, a rural dean. In both professions, he was able to exercise, to the greatest advantage of all those who came in contact with this sunny man, gold all through, his natural gifts of communication and his completely uninhibited sense of joy.

I am aware that much of this may read like a Prize-Giving in reverse, a Speech Day in which the prizes are being awarded by the Ruined Boys to their teachers. But I have not finished yet. Nor, I hope, will I ever finish acknowledging the advice, help, inspiration, and information I have received from others : my parents, my masters, my school-fellows, my French *maîtres*, French local historians, fellow researchers, and my own students and graduates. For a historian is someone who can never profitably work in complete isolation; and so much good history has been knocked together, in conversations in the little café, *Le Petit Berri*, rue des Francs-Bourgeois, directly opposite the entrance to the Archives Nationales, as historians, of various nationalities, fresh from the excitements of a day in the Hôtel Soubise, tell one another of their discoveries.

So I do not feel the need to apologise for the biggest prize I still have to award.

I have had a great deal of luck in my life, not the least in the guidance that I received, as a young researcher, from General Herlaut and from Pierre Caron, then the Directeur des Archives de France. But the greatest stroke of luck came my way, in a typically accidental manner, in my second year at Shrewsbury. The history master at the time had been George Rudé's Housemaster; and he was the expert on the Dangers of Up River. I do not think that he gave as much attention to history as he did to the activities of nude boys, though he was an acknowledged international expert on bindings. Most of his finest pieces have been kept in the school library. But bindings were not a particularly inspiring introduction to human history. And under the administration of this master, the History Sixth had acquired a justified reputation for being a comfortable backwater : *otium cum dignitate* was its motto.

But, in mid-term, in my second year, it was suddenly announced that the history master had had some sort of breakdown, and had had to give up both his form and his House, certainly a double benefit, because Mr Sopwith took over the latter. We were perhaps pretty knowing boys in matters concerning ourselves, but we must have been singularly innocent in those concerning masters. For, on hearing of this sudden revolution in our affairs, we all attributed it to alcoholism. It was only much later, when I was at Oxford, and met the boy who had been the innocent cause of this dramatic affair at a party in Magdalen, that I learnt the full details of what then became known as The Regent Palace Incident. The history master had long been in the habit of organising reading parties, taking, for the summer holidays, a selected group of boys—the selection seems to have been primarily on looks—to a chalet that he possessed in the Swiss Alps. These excursions had apparently gone off, for years, without any untoward incident : or those who had gone on them had maintained a prudent silence. But, in the end, temptation had proved too strong. The master and the boys returned from Switzerland, and were spending a night in the Regent Palace Hotel, before dispersing. There had been a scene in a bedroom; and the boy concerned had effected his escape, telephoning his parents from the reception desk downstairs.

This master was replaced by a temporary master, J. R. M. Senior, who came to us straight from Christ Church, where he had just taken schools. Mr Senior lost no time in taking in hand the History Side. It was no longer *otium cum dignitate*, but hard work, wonderful teaching, and, very soon, sensational results, so sensational that even the Head-master became convinced that history was, after all, a worth while subject, and that boys of promise should not be discouraged from going

on to the History Side. I went to see Mr Senior, in his digs in Canon-
bury—a room with a fine view over the walls and spires of the town
(later he lived in a strange Elizabethan brick manor house, at the far
end of the town, near the Abbey church)—and told him that I wanted
to become a historian. Instead of pointing out the difficulties, he did
everything to encourage me; and, as he was a firm, not to say obstinate
man, he eventually had his way both with the Headmaster, and with
my old enemy at No. 1 the Schools. I still think that the first time I
found myself securely seated in the History Side, a small narrow room,
separated from Maths by a partition wall—and it was an uncomfortable
proximity, for while the History Side was always extremely noisy (Mr
Brooke's French lessons were anything but quiet, and the periods with
the Latin master, Mr Dawson, must have sounded like a Punch-and-Judy
show) the Maths Side was as quiet as the grave—its walls covered with
prints of Shropshire churches and castles, a relic of the deposed master,
was the happiest day I have ever spent. For now I knew that I could
concentrate on history, that I could amputate myself, cut myself off
from anything that was not in some way related to history, give myself
over entirely to the joys of learning more and more history. Mr Senior,
whose enormously impressive profile caused him to be known as 'the
Iron Duke', was more of a tutor than a schoolmaster. We went, in pairs,
to read him essays at his home : an activity doubly attractive, because
it got us out of our Houses at night—we were given sherry, and Mr
Senior would comment, always, so it seemed to me, with great skill and
imagination, on what we had read to him, getting the other boy to
say what he thought. He was, too, highly intelligent in the way that he
paired us; for a long time, I was coupled with Brian Inglis, a Dubliner,
who wrote extremely well, and always had far more ideas that I did. I
tried to make up the balance on information, on having read more than
Brian. He was interested in ideas, I was concerned with political narrative; he favoured the broad sweep and general comparisons, I preferred
the detailed study of political machines; he was idealistic, and I affected
what I imagined to be an eighteenth-century cynicism, for, already,
under Mr Senior, I had become a total convert to that elegant and
unenthusiastic scene. Our history master indulged all of us in our particular enthusiasms, and made of a History Side of eight boys a permanent,
exciting, and endlessly rewarding centre of debate and wonder. Perhaps
the only time that he attempted to impose his own ideas upon us was
when he eagerly tried to convert us to the merits of Georgism. He had
been converted to *Progress and Poverty*, while in Peckwater, of all places,
rather as if one had discovered the light of Marx while in the long
gallery of the Vatican. On the subject of Henry George, the apostle of

social credit, he was implacable; we had to accept the Truth, and did, to escape further indoctrination.

He was also concerned to make us aware of what was happening in Europe in the early 1930s. We each had to make a weekly report on the area assigned to us. I can remember reporting on the Spanish elections of 1934, so that Gil Roblès became a familiar, if loathed, figure to me. We were encouraged to illustrate these reports with photographs cut out of the papers. There was one of the girls of the *Folies Bergères* wearing masks representing the faces of the current French government: one very tall girl (*la Grande Perche*) hidden behind the long face of Pierre-Etienne Flandin, another, dumpy girl displaying the strangely Asiatic features and white tie of Pierre Laval. There was even a female hiding behind the melancholy, jaundiced—literally jaundiced—face of Georges Bonnet. I thought such frivolity rather shocking. Mr Senior also saw to it that we were given an opportunity of reading the weekly bulletin put out by the Soviet Embassy, then under the rather amiable Ivan Maisky. He showed us caricatures, read us skits, taking off the ineffable Ramsay Macdonald, who by then must have been clearly on the way to madness. I suppose that Mr Senior might have been considered a man of the Left; the only time that I ever saw him completely lose his temper with us was when one of us, in order to test his reactions, proposed that Oswald Mosley should be invited to address the 1918 Society, which was the school contemporary history body. Later, during the war, he became something of an English nationalist, taking it out of the Americans, and with what I considered a very healthy dislike of the Irish. He upbraided me when I told him how much I warmed to the inhabitants of the valleys of South Wales, when I was stationed there as a soldier. But he never had anything against the Scots, indeed marrying one, a musical girl from Rumbling Bridge. But whatever he was, he enthralled us, filled us with a sense of wonder, taking us right out of the fuggy isolation of Kingsland and its inbred, tribal *mores.* Certainly when we left school we were all vaguely pro-Soviet—we were also shown edifying Soviet films about railway construction and that sort of thing (I remember one occasion when the serious intent of Soviet propaganda was rather lost, on the appearance of a caption, on a film about the building of some Asiatic line, *Frozen Banks,* which provoked an uproar of mirth, for whatever might be said about the incandescent Captain Banks, he was anything but that) in the Alington Hall—and I think we were also quite healthily anti-fascist, without, however, any strong sense of political commitment and purposefulness. There was too much basic frivolity in most of us, and, indeed, in the whole climate of the school, the Liverpool Unitarians excepted—for they were a dull lot, as well as bullies—for any of us ever to have thought that the future of mankind somehow lay with us. Clover's answers to his Certificate A paper met with universal commendations, even from boys who were going into the Army, and, a year after I left, one of the Dubliners had a broadsheet printed, then dropped from a hired aeroplane over Kingsland, carrying the message: THE SHADOW OF MILITARISM HANGS OVER SHREWSBURY SCHOOL. We did not regard it as our destiny to lead politically; *Private Eye*, created by Salopians, did not then exist, but the irreverent and frivolous spirit that lay behind its creation was already there.

But my own greatest debt to the Duke was the discovery of Namier. Now here was a level of history the existence of which I had never previously suspected. I was absolutely enthralled by his use of the minutiae of personal case histories, and it seemed to me that he was a historian who was writing about real people, about human beings and not just about Heroes, great principles, ideas, and that sort of thing. I delighted above all in his portrayal of the great Duke of Newcastle, for me the very quintessence of the anti-hero, a personage of delightfully unglorious proportions (my previous anti-Hero had been *The Trimmer,* Halifax, and, to this day, I have reserved a partiality for statesmen skilled in the art of survival in difficult and violent times). Namier brought history down to a new, fascinating level in another way as well. I could not fail to be deeply excited by his chapter on the Shropshire gentry of the eighteenth century: the member for Shrewsbury, the member for Bridgnorth, the member for Bishop's Castle, and so on: for here were the names of our school governors, the Offley-Wakemans of this small world, here too the names of the current Members of Parliament for the county, families that had been in the House of Commons for at least two centuries. It was a wonderful lesson in the continuity of history. And it was immensely exhilarating to discover that there was this completely unexplored angle to English history, as witnessed from the halls of Shropshire landowners, many of which I regularly passed on my solitary runs, rather than from Westminster. Namier did for me, as a schoolboy, what Hoskins later did for so many others. He took me away from the purely national scene and reminded me that politics and political management were about local issues and local interests; and he taught me the immense importance of regionalism. I have always considered myself a local historian, and have derived the greatest pleasure in researching on and writing about French local history. When I went to Oxford, my medieval history tutor, Idris Dean Jones, soon discovering my *penchant,* encouraged me to approach thirteenth-, fourteenth- and fifteenth-century English history in terms of the March. 'Forget about London,' he would say, 'imagine that you are in Gloucester, or Hereford, or Ludlow, or Chester, and you will find that it will all fall into place.' I became quite a pundit on the marriage alliances of the de Clares and the Mortimers, and, at Merton, enjoyed English One, as well as the lectures of Bruce Macfarlane on the de la Poles and the Beauchamps, all of which I attended, more than any other period. This I owed entirely to the Duke's communicated enthusiasm for Namier. I also owed to Namier and the Duke the fact that, in 1934, I won Dr Bright's History Prize, the subject of which, that year, was 'Party Politics under George II'. Just after leaving school, and before going to Paris, I obtained a reader's ticket—I was seventeen at the time —to the Manuscript Room of the British Museum, spending some weeks working on the Newcastle Papers, enjoying every bit of it, especially His Grace's diligence in replying to letters and in expressing his thanks for the gift of such closely related things as a brace of pheasants or a Suffolk living. This was concrete history, not a lot of airy-fairy stuff about ideas. It was from the Duke and Jane Austen, read with admiring devotion in the school library, that I acquired my delight in everything connected with the eighteenth century. The great Lord Hervey and his marvellously chiselled malice—and malice is the literary form I have always most admired—would later complete my education, along with Lord Chesterfield, Wilkes and *Junius*.

But the Duke's influence extended far beyond these familiar land-marks. I remember that on one occasion he took me to see an American historical film about Catherine the Great. And among the books I chose for the Bright Prize were Trotsky's *History of the Russian Revolution*, Low's *Russian Sketchbook* (the product of a visit to the Soviet Union in the company of Kingsley Martin), an attractive nineteenth-century edition of Clarendon (another survivor), an abridged edition of Pepys, and, for some unearthly reason, *The Testament of Beauty*, by the current Poet Laureate, Robert Bridges. I cannot say that I have ever read it. But it was elegantly bound, like the books left to the school by the Duke's accident-prone predecessor.

I suspect that the Duke really believed in the Broad Sweep approach to history and that he liked dealing in centuries, worlds and continents. He certainly had little sympathy for what he regarded as narrow specialisation, and later he reproached me for using up my time and substance on anything as parochial as a few years of the French Revolu-tion. But he was far too honest a historian, too good and scrupulous a teacher to fall for Patterns and Cycles and the over-facile interpretations of exponents of comparative history, and he rendered us all a good service in warning us against Toynbee's *A Study of History*, which he rightly regarded, not as bad history, but as anti-history. He pointed out to us the many inaccuracies in the book. Peter the Great, for instance, was packed off on his European trip five or ten years too early, in order to

suit the dictates of the strangely sexual theme of Withdrawal and Return.
We were thus inoculated against the dangers of infection from Germanic
wave cycles. I can picture his mirth when confronted with R. R. Palmer's
geo-political Atlantic Time Machine, and with his obsession with the
year 1760. Here, for instance, was the English female domestic servant
—milady's parlourmaid—going to bed on 31 December 1759, and
waking up on 1 January 1760 a Girl Reborn. He would have been
quick to laugh this sort of pretentious nonsense out of court. In short,
he was a great lover of truth, as well as an inspiring teacher.

Such was the Duke's ability as a teacher of history, and as a tutor,
that of the eight boys who formed the History Side in my last year,
seven of us won open awards at Oxford and Cambridge colleges. And
this spanking pace was to be kept up during the following years, until
the day, a sad one for Shrewsbury, he left, to take up a headmastership.
We were extraordinarily lucky in thus being among the first pupils of
this remarkable, gifted and, above all, enthusiastic man, happily still
teaching, though officially retired, now at Harrow. I do not know how
many historical vocations began under his exciting impetus; but I can
mention, *en passant*, Brian Inglis and Maurice Craig. I am not sure
whether he ever quite forgave me for deserting English history for that
of France. He disliked Europeans almost as much as he detested the Irish
and the Americans; and he must have thought that I had discovered a
mightily strange bed-fellow in the self-righteous Robespierre. He was, of
course, quite right; but it took me several years to discover this for
myself.

Murray Senior was then my major good fortune, just as much as
my Housemaster was my—indeed our—major misfortune. But there
were other masters too who did what they could for me. Often, it was
not very much. I was the despair of successive mathematics masters, and,
in science periods, only succeeded in burning myself or in breaking the
equipment owing to my clumsiness. Frank Macarthy, as he then was,
vainly tried to instil in me some simple notions of biology, but he was
rather more successful in his other role as a teacher of Divinity. He was
gentle, quietly humorous, patient, and very very wise. And luckily this
was not the last I saw of him. The Headmaster, Mr Hardy, also helped
to make me appreciate the splendid language of the Old Testament, as
well as the beauty of the Shropshire hills. Under rather a severe exterior,
he was a kindly, compassionate man who, during the War, took infinite
trouble to keep up with former members of the school who were serving
in the Forces.

In December 1934, I went to Oxford, to sit for the Christ Church
group, putting Merton—on purely aesthetic grounds, though as it turned

out it was an extremely happy decision on every possible count—as the College of my first choice. Mr Senior told me not to worry too much, it was merely a trial run, I could always have another go in the following March. He also suggested that, while I was about it, I might as well stay on in Oxford a further week, and try for Worcester, then, for some reason, on its own. The prospect of nearly a fortnight away from school naturally appealed to me, and I very willingly took on the extra commitment. Several of us from Shrewsbury turned up in Christ Church Hall for the first paper. Near our table, there was a tall, swarthy boy, rather pallid, who looked about thirty, and who was talking loudly, confidently, and knowingly, about various dons, referring to them by their Christian names. 'Of course,' we heard him saying, 'any reference to Namier will dish you with Keith'; I did not then know that the Keith in question was Keith Feiling, but so much inside knowledge did seem infinitely demoralising, and I had put so much of my money on Namier. I remember whispering to one of my companions : 'I think we had better go straight back to Shrewsbury, we are just not in this team.' But we stuck it out. On the second or third day of the papers, I discovered that the boy's name was Philip Toynbee.

I was interviewed in one of the Merton Common Rooms, by two elderly dons from Univ.; they were very urbane and seemed quite exquisitely polite, listening to me carefully, and making such flattering comments as 'That is very interesting', as though they really meant it. They asked me to tell them the manner of Edward II's death, and this I did, blushing scarlet. But, above all, they complimented me on my knowledge of eighteenth-century English history. This made me quite cheerful. I was staying in a room occupied by an undergraduate with the splendid name of Royal-Dawson. I went through his bookshelves, and devoured a very moving book by an American, about convalescing from a serious illness in a nursing home with a view of trees and hilly woodlands. I enjoyed the stillness of the scene. I went to a cinema in Queen Street, and saw a film in which a fourteen-year-old Wendy Hiller succeeded in bringing back together her estranged parents; on the newsreel, there were pictures of British troops leaving for the Saar.

At the week-end, I moved to Worcester, and was given a very handsome room in the eighteenth-century part of the College, overlooking the sunken quadrangle. I spent some time reading Trotsky and going for walks on Shotover. The following week, I sat the Worcester papers in a Hall covered in dark panelling bearing crests. On the last day of the exam, I was sent for by the History tutor; he, too, seemed elderly, and was also exquisitely polite. He told me that he had just heard that I had been awarded the History Postmastership at Merton, and that my name would be up on a list in the Lodge there. And he added that he was sorry that I was not coming to Worcester—which was a very kind thing for him to say. He was, however, wrong.

I walked to Merton in the December night, as on air. And there was my name, just legible, underneath that of Arthur Peterson, who had got a Postmastership in Classics, both written in a trembling hand, on a piece of torn-out graph paper, by Warden Bowman, then in his late eighties, and in his sixty-fifth year in Merton.

The next morning, I telegraphed my Headmaster and my Housemaster, packed up, leaving Worcester with a raging toothache, to take the train to Tunbridge Wells. Nearly thirty-nine years later, I returned to Worcester, as a Fellow, soon occupying the rooms I still have, on the other side of the sunken quadrangle, in one of the medieval cottages. It was rather like moving from George II to Henry VI. But, for a journey that had taken nearly forty years, I had not moved very far in space. I have no doubt that Professor Palmer and historians of his kind would have found some neat pattern, some tidy message, in my journey *aller et retour*. All I can find in it is the happy intervention of chance. There might, too, be some logic in this move away from the Meadows and towards the station; for I had followed, though not on the tow path, the direction of the Merton versus Worcester public house bicycle race, in which I had previously competed, predictably falling into the Isis. Whatever interpretation one can put on this example of social mobility —a theme with which I have been very much concerned in my most recent book[1]—I had, as it were, *bouclé la boucle*. And this sounds as satisfying as it is in reality.

When I went to Manchester, as a Senior Simon Research Fellow, I was soon followed there by Tito's official biographer, the former Partisan General, Vlado Dedijer, who had taken up his fellowship in order to write two books, the one on Serbian nationalism between 1900 and 1914, the other on the origins, motivations, and personnel of Sarajevo. He had been a journalist before the war, spending some time in London as correspondent of *Politika*. And although he had made an excellent job of *Tito Speaks,* he did not regard himself as a qualified historian. On his arrival in Manchester, he came to see me, asking me what was the best method to follow in order to become a historian. What methodological equipment should he acquire? I shocked him very much by saying that no such method existed, that the methodology of history was the invention of solemn Germans and was the ruination, as future historians, of the unfortunate pupils at the Normal School of Pisa. One just went to the records, read them, thought about them, read some more, and the records would do the rest, they would dictate the exact limits of the

---

[1] *Paris and its Provinces* (London 1975).

subject, and provide both inspiration and material. All the historian had
to do was to be able to read, and, above all, to write clearly and agreeably. I could see that he was very shocked. There must, he objected, be
a methodology of history that had to be mastered before one tackled
history itself. I would have none of this and he gave me up in despair,
as an incurable amateur and pragmatist. Of course, I had not wished
to discourage him; on the contrary, I pointed out to him that he was
unusually well-equipped to deal with both his subjects as he was himself
a Bosnian, as he had been dangled on the knee of Colonel 'Apis', an
intimate friend of his father, as, shortly after the Liberation of Yugo-
slavia, Tito had entrusted him with the task of assembling material for
the rehabilitation of 'Apis' and the other members of the Black Hand,
and, finally, as he was a natural writer. So he went to Gerald Aylmer,
to get a second opinion. And Gerald told him much the same thing.
He did eventually write *The Road to Sarajevo*, without encumbering
himself with methodology, and leaving his Marxism in the cloakroom;
it is an excellent and very readable book.

But I did not tell Vlado the worst : that one never *became* a historian.
I am still becoming one. This is not as discouraging as it sounds, for it
is the process of becoming, like the process of research itself—delving
into a new box, untying the bundles—that is so enjoyable, and so rewarding. It is better to live on in expectancy, than to sit back and contemplate
the static scene of fulfilment. At Shrewsbury I was becoming, and I am
still becoming. It has been a constantly exciting, exhilarating journey up
till now, as fresh and as full of wonder as in the small room at the far
end of the school buildings, an eighteenth-century workhouse, presided
over by the medallion-like, leonine profile of the Iron Duke.

PART II

'L'Affaire Perken':
A Double Murder on the
Franco-Dutch Border, 1809

'L'Affaire Perken'

...que de ces trois individus il y en avait deux grands, et un plus petit, que les deux premiers sont vêtus de gilets ronds à manches de drap bleu, de pantalons bleus de la même étoffe, le troisième un gilet bleu, pantalon blanc, un gros mouchoir blanc au col, et tous les trois des casquettes de cuir, paraissant être marins, le plus grand a sur le bras gauche un signe picqué et brûlé avec de la poudre, le petit a une cicatrice sur la joue, et qui parlent tous trois hollandais et ont des passeports, l'un pour Turnhout, et les autres pour Lierre en Westphalie. (*Archives Nationales* BB 18 571, Justice, Deux-Nèthes, procès-verbal dressé par le commissaire de police de la première Section de la Ville d'Anvers, 28 July 1809)

...que vendredi soir du 21 juillet de cette année...entre 9h. et 10h. les déposants se sont trouvés sur la route de Rosendaal, que trois hommes sont passés près d'eux, dont deux étaient plus grands que le troisième, en veste, pantalon, & ayant des casquettes sur la tête, dirigeant leurs pas près de la maison du forgeron van Leen vers la route dite *Bugweg* qui conduit à Steenbergen, que lesdites personnes paraissaient être pressées, mettant beaucoup de célérité dans leur marche. (*Ibid.*, déposition devant le bailli de Steenbergen de deux habitants de Kruisland, 16 October 1809)

...que le samedi 22...Juillet...environ 3h. et demi du matin, deux hommes inconnus se sont rendus au domicile de sa mère, la veuve Stellemaar ...qu'ils étaient en veste bleu & petit gilet à fleurs, de longues culottes soit pantalon brun, des souliers pointus et ayant des casquettes sur la tête...un troisième inconnu...n'était pas de grande taille, ayant une veste bleue, longue culotte, soit pantalon blanc, et de même une casquette sur la tête. (*Ibid.*, déposition d'Angelina Cornelia Stellemaar, épouse van Weizel, 27 September 1809)

...que le samedi 22...environ 6h. après-midi lui déposant s'est trouvé au lieu nommé Sas ou Stoofdijk sur la hauteur entre le Hoetje étant loué ou affermé à Marquis Bevelande [sic] et l'endroit nommé *Kammeke,* lui déposant étant en cabriolet tiré par un seul cheval, lui portant des lunettes, et qu'à côté de lui était à cheval le nommé Ebert Joan Dewert, qu'au bas de la digue ils ont rencontré trois hommes en veste bleue, ayant de longues et larges culottes flamèches et des casquettes sur la tête...que lui déposant et led. Sr. Dewert causant ensemble sur cette rencontre se dirent qu'ils les prenaient pour des matelots, attendu leur costume. (*Ibid.*, déposition de Pieter Deneve, 10 October 1809)

...que dans l'après-midi du samedi 22 du présent mois...vers les 6h. étant venus à la maison soit auberge de sa mère trois hommes inconnus... le plus grand... avait sur le bras gauche une marque en piqures formant quelques figures qui avaient été brûlés et frottés avec de la poudre à canon selon l'usage des marins... ils ont dit qu'ils étaient pressés, car qu'ils devaient se rendre en Zélande. (*Ibid.*, déposition de Jan Neyssen, demeurant au Zevente, Ruyte, 25 July 1809)

... sur les 7h. est venue dans le jardin... par lui habité Elisabeth Aarts... laquelle vint acheter du beurre chez son épouse... elle raconta... qu'il lui était survenu des passagers auxquels elle devait donner à manger, à coucher, ajoutant que c'étaient des jeunes gaillards dont elle n'avait pas grande opinion. (*Ibid.*, déposition de Johannes van Hoof, paysan, 11 October 1809)

Notendaal was a hamlet that has perhaps since disappeared, as it is no longer marked on the map. According to the numerous and varied testimony available to us, much of it illustrating a painter's skill in physical observation, it consisted of a few isolated houses and two white-walled inns with roofs in red tiles, lying below the level of a network of dikes, in rich corn land cut by a series of small streams, and connected by little bridges. In an area so low-lying, the passer-by, on foot or on horseback, could be seen from afar, silhouetted against the summer sun, on the top of a dike or raised road or sea-wall. He would not be seen once, *en passant*, but several times, and by many watchful eyes, as the pattern of paths and tracks between the ditches and waterways forced him along a predictable, because fixed, course. The possibility of wandering off-track was limited, the opportunity to hide, or *prendre la couleur du paysage,* would be almost non-existent. In a peasant community, and in an area of rich grainlands, people would be afoot before dawn, by half past three or four in the morning; and as an English invasion of Tholen was expected, there was fairly heavy horse and waggon traffic along the tops of the dikes throughout much of the night.

Notendaal seems to have been about half-way between Steenbergen, a small town connected to the estuary dividing Schouwen and Overflakke from the mainland, and the village of Kruisland. Steenbergen at the time had a garrison of the Dutch artillery that in the previous year had been stationed at Burghsluis, a small port near the tip of Schouwen. It also had a court, presided over by a *bailli*. The nearest important centres were Rosendaal and Bergen-op-Zoom. Due west lay the estuary of the West Schelde and the island of Tholen. One of the mouths of the Maas was situated less than three miles to the north. It was thus almost a coastal area, offering, at least as far as Schouwen and Tholen were concerned, the possibility of invasion by small English forces. It was also an ancient border area between the United Provinces and the Austrian

Netherlands, the former at this time the Kingdom of Holland, and the latter incorporated into the French Empire. The nearest point on the frontier was at Essen, about six miles south of Notendaal, on the road from Rosendaal to Antwerp, ten miles to the south. This part of what had been Brabant now formed the Département des Deux-Nèthes, the central criminal court of which was in the *chef-lieu*, Antwerp. The border ran, in a series of loops, from west to east, starting from the mouth of the Schelde just north of Zandvliet, eastwards through Putte, Essen, Meerle, Hoogstraten, Poppel, just south of Tilburg, and then southwards in the direction of Belgian Limburg. A few years earlier, the judicial authorities of the Deux-Nèthes had frequently complained of the activities of gangs of smugglers to the north of Antwerp, while Antwerp itself, under the Directory, had had the reputation, at least with the disenchanted French authorities, of being both a smugglers' paradise and a centre for anti-French feeling. In the last five years of the previous century, the Isle of Axel, on the far side of the Schelde estuary, had been a favoured landing place for smuggled English goods, as well as an area of endemic banditry centred on Ghent.[1] In all this border area, strangers, especially those travelling at dusk or very early in the morning, whether on horseback or on foot, were likely, no doubt rightly, to be regarded with suspicion by farmers, peasants, and innkeepers. Not that the latter were particularly law-abiding, many of them acting as receivers for smugglers known to them. Men on foot would appear more suspicious than men on horseback; a single walker might be written off as a scout, but three men walking together would necessarily attract notice, and inspire fear.

Sailors would of course be familiar figures in such a region. But such familiarity would not breed reassurance, especially in time of war. And Dutch sailors seem to have been the source of even greater alarm in their own coastal areas than French sailors were to the authorities of Le Havre and Dieppe. There was no mistaking a sailor, both by the way he walked, and by the clothes he wore: straw hats or leather caps, blue jackets, wide blue or white trousers, black pointed shoes, with buckles. There were other tell-tale signs, such as tattoos on the arm—in blue and red, representing an anchor, a marine monster, a naked girl, or a girl's name —a gold ring through one ear, and, in this border area, a readiness to offer, or to accept, *la goutte* : a glass of *genièvre*. These visible signs might be confirmed by a certain boisterous joviality, a propensity to engage in conversation with the first-comer, whether in the easy affability of the road, or in the immediate *bonhomie* of the wayside inn. Sailors and fishermen, unlike peasants, have always had the reputation of being talkative and gregarious, though much of their talkativeness may have

[1] R. C. Cobb, *Paris and its Provinces* (London, 1975), ch. 5, 'La bande juive'.

also been designed to reassure those whom they met. They would, for instance, be very ready with information about their movements: 'We have come from Holland', 'We have walked thirteen leagues from Tilburg', 'We are heading for Zeeland to sign up on a privateer', even when no one had asked them the nature of their business.

So there seems to have been no doubt as to their occupation in the minds of the many local people, most of them inhabitants of Kruisland, who, at one time or another, in the full light of day, in the half-light of dusk, or even before dawn, in the pitch black momentarily illuminated by an open door or the flame of a pipe being lit, had caught sight of the three travellers. Nearly all were to make the point that they were dressed like sailors, even that they appeared to *be* sailors. A number exchanged greetings with them on the road, or bantered with them in inns. There was no doubt therefore that they were Dutch, though two of them spoke with the unfamiliar accent of Friesland. The third, who was the biggest, and the most noticeable, the one all would remember first, because his left arm was tattooed, because he did most of the talking, may have aroused less curiosity, because he spoke like the locals. All three did, however, inspire a considerable degree of curiosity, even of speculation. The woman whom they knocked up at half past three in the morning, asking for a light, would not let them in, and noticed, perhaps with alarm, that one of them was standing back from the others, as though to avoid the light, or as if he were acting as a scout. But she did not wish to antagonise them, explaining that they could not come in lest they wake up her child. A man, on being told by the innkeeper's wife that she had three young men staying the night at her place, decided to go over and have a look at them. He found them informative enough, the one with the local accent even claiming, though he could not recall the fact, that they had met a year or so before. The man in glasses, travelling in a gig, and his companion, riding beside him on horseback, after meeting them coming the other way, along the top of the dike, and being greeted by them as they doffed their caps, went on talking about their encounter, as they made their way home for supper on that July evening. Perhaps there was not much to talk about, if one lived in Kruisland or Steenbergen, even though there was a garrison in the small town. Perhaps, too, country people were naturally affable; or, equally, there may have been a reason for this sort of formal politeness, the exchange of greetings, the doffing of headgear, for to make the traveller speak out clearly was halfway to identification—it could spell the difference between a stranger and a foreigner—and it would be easier to recognise, and to memorise, the faces of those who had taken off their caps. A great many people were subsequently to recognise the three walkers, even though, in most cases, they had only encountered them briefly. The man in glasses and his companion had no doubt in their minds that the three were sailors; and there were plenty of reasons for sailors to be out and about, and on the move, in this coastal area, at a time when an English landing seemed imminent. But what might have aroused suspicion was that the travellers, unlike sailors who were about to rejoin their ships, or who were on shore leave, were not carrying their tin *cantines*, nor even a bundle, were in fact empty-handed.

There are hints too, in much of the copious evidence available, that in their bright colours—blue jackets, white trousers, red neckties, brown caps, their pointed, shiny shoes, white neckerchiefs tied up high over the throat, all indicating a rather *voyant* concern for elegance—and in their contrasting appearance, two of them very tall, and striding out as if they were well used to life on the road, or were in a great hurry to reach a place or to get away from another one, the other very short, tubby, and apparently having difficulty in keeping up with his companions, they may also have been the object of a certain amount of rustic amusement. The inhabitants of Kruisland would not have much to laugh about, and countrymen are quick to make fun of urban display and boastfulness. Certainly, all the witnesses insist first of all on the contrast between the tall pair and their short companion. There is a very ancient appeal about the old military joke on the subject of the long, the short, and the tall, and as they made their way, in their elegant pointed shoes, the two tall ones smoking pipes, they must have been vaguely reminiscent of a couple of Quixotes, accompanied by a Sancho, or whatever would be the equivalent in the fairground humour of a Dutch peasant. But the short man also seems to have been the object of fears difficult to express : several witnesses mention that he had a scar running down his left cheek. The other two might have been friends or travelling companions, but the presence of the third man seemed vaguely sinister, if only because he seemed the odd man out. Small men are thought to be dangerous, as well as comical, especially small men with scars. And a number of witnesses were to recall, some six months later, that while *les deux jeunes gaillards* had shown themselves in the open, coming forward with the ready joke of the early nineteenth-century walking traveller, their companion had tended to lurk in the background, had kept his hat on in the inn, or had remained silent. Perhaps they had not chosen his company; perhaps it had in some way been *imposed* upon them. It looked to several as if they had been unable to shake off the little man with the tell-tale scar.

These, then, were the appearances, and they were appearances on which all the witnesses were to enlarge. Yet they seem to have been deceptive. The tallest of the three, who to all those who had met them seemed to be the leader—it was he who did the talking, he that made the jokes, and he who spoke in the local dialect—had, it is true, at the time of his arrest, described himself as a sailor. But this was the only time he did, though the tattoos may have given away more than he would have wished. We know in fact almost for certain that the travellers were *not* sailors, that they had probably never been to sea, save possibly as children, for they would not have had time to go to sea, even though two of them came from Leeuwarden, in Friesland, and one of these had parents who made nets for the fishing fleet. For one reason or another, they wanted to *appear* to be sailors, dressing as such, even taking care, in one of their stops on the other side of the frontier, to purchase three round hats, in order to make their part as Honest Jacks more convincing; their clothes were a form of disguise, and not a very intelligent one, but as we shall see they were very stupid people. Their clothes may also have been the visible affirmation of an intention, for it seems likely that two of them at least had headed across the frontier in order to enlist on a French privateer; they even knew the name of a captain of such a ship, de Vries. However, if they dressed like sailors, they were almost insistent, in their conversations as reported in inns, that they had in fact served with the Dutch army, and that they were travelling to take up any job that they could find in their own trades: the two tall fellows as carpenters, Kroes as a *garçon brasseur*.[1]

It is time then to look beyond appearances and to state in detail what we know of the three travellers, of their past, and of their activities. It might be simplest to begin at the end of what was quite a long journey, and from which there could be no return. For, on Wednesday 28 February 1810, the three travelling companions were hanged, one after the other, on the square opposite the town hall of Steenbergen. Despite a number of not very convincing lies concerning Christian names, place and date of birth, there is little mystery about the three young men, and about what had brought them to the place of execution. We even have a detailed, almost hour-by-hour knowledge of their itinerary in their last ten days of freedom.

The tallest of the three, and the one who seems to have been acknowledged as leader by the others, at least as far as their last operation was concerned, gave his name, at the time of his arrest in Antwerp, as Cornelis Perken, aged twenty, a bachelor, and describing himself as

[1] They told Adriaan Mes, while at the Notendaal inn, 'qu'ils devaient partir le lendemain de grand matin, car qu'ils allaient en Zélande, que deux d'entr'eux étaient charpentiers, et le troisième garçon brasseur, lequel était plus gros que les autres'. This must have been something that Perken had thought up there and then, no doubt to fit Kroes' tubby appearance: he must have *looked* like a brewer. Hofman, as we know, was in fact a goldsmith, Kroes had at one time been trained as a tailor. See below, pp. 57–8.

'un matelot venant d'Amsterdam'. Perken went on to say that his birth-place was Hilvarenbeek, a village in the county of Bois-le-Duc, just south of Tilburg and very close to the French frontier. He would thus have been born in 1789. His parents, Pieter Perken and Getrud van Es, had been peasants, and he thought that they were still alive in 1809, though he had not seen them for some time. When he had last had news of them, they were employed on a farm at Moergestel, a village three miles to the east of Hilvarenbeek. But, on 15 February 1810, a little before his execution, he confessed to the *bailli* and *échevins* of Steenbergen that he had in fact been born in this same village, Moergestel, not in Hilvaren-beek, and that he had been baptised Anthony, and not Cornelis. The reason for this rather pathetic subterfuge, which consisted in displacing his place of birth two or three miles, and of altering his Christian name, seems to have been his desire to spare his parents the knowledge of a previous conviction and of his impending execution. Like the other two, he appears to have been a dutiful son, and he was to tell the Antwerp *commissaire* that he had been anxious to keep his most recent activities secret from his parents; as far as they were concerned, he was still serving in the Dutch artillery. He had been brought up and remained a Catholic. Perken was the one with the tattoo design on his left arm, and, accord-ing to the others—and this seems very likely, in view of his origins—he was the only one familiar with the Steenbergen area and the border country. At the time of his arrest, the *commissaire* undressed him, and was quick to discover that he had been branded on the right shoulder and that his back was marked by a flogging : undeniable evidence of a previous conviction. He went on to say that, although he had been brought up to be a peasant, he had enlisted as a young man, serving four or five years. For a long time, he was strenuously to deny ever having been in the Rosendaal–Steenbergen area between 20 and 22 July 1809, adding that he had come to Antwerp to enlist on a privateer that he believed to be in the harbour, giving de Vries as the name of its captain. Perken was illiterate, signing his final statement with a cross.

The second man of the trio, also tall, also a Catholic, gave his name as Christian Hofman, and, at first, his age as twenty-three (later, on the eve of his execution, he changed this to twenty-five, an age more feasible, as he had previously stated that he had served some six years in the army). He was thus the oldest of the three. He was born in Leeuwarden, in Friesland, where his parents, whom he believed to be still alive, worked as *noueurs de filets*. He himself, however, had been trained as a gold-smith, his parents having wished to see him better his position; and, at the time of his arrest, he had already parted company with the other two—he was caught at Westmalle, on his way to Hoogstraten, where, so he said, he had hoped to find employment in his trade. He certainly had a knowledge of jewellery and precious metals denied to his companions; and he was the only one of the three to be able at least to sign his name. Once undressed, he too was found to have the tell-tale marks of a previous branding and flogging; these he attributed, without much conviction, to an illness. Like Perken, he was unmarried.

The third traveller was the little man with a scar on his left cheek who had caused so much alarm to all those who had encountered the trio. He gave his name as Jan Kroes, and his age as twenty-four. Like Hofman, he had been born in Leeuwarden, but, unlike the other two, he had been brought up and had remained a member of the Dutch Reformed Church. His parents, whom he thought were still alive—he had not seen them for nine months—and were living in Leeuwarden, were tailors, and he had been brought up in that trade, before enlisting in the army. He had remained at home till the age of thirteen, and had always been well treated by his parents. He was a member of a large family, with four brothers, one of them older than he, and one sister. Although he had attended Protestant services, he had never had any formal religious education. Stripped, he too was discovered to have been branded and flogged at a fairly recent date. His interrogators were not long in discovering that, despite his alarming appearance, he was in fact the weak link in the group; they caught him out in a whole chain of contradictions on the subject of the itinerary that the men had followed. Like Perken, he seems to have been rather stupid. He, too, was a bachelor.

Perken and Kroes were arrested in Antwerp, place Verte, near the cemetery. Arrested with them was a fourth personage, who had been drinking and eating with them, and at their expense, in the course of the previous day or two. He gave his name as Jan Jannssens, his age as twenty-nine. He was not a Dutchman, and lived in Antwerp, working as a *faiseur de peignes*. He was illegitimate, did not know his place of birth, had been an *enfant de troupe,* then a soldier in the Austrian army. He also described himself as a *journalier*. After questioning him, the *commissaire* was easily convinced by his story that he had fallen in with the trio while drinking in an Antwerp wineshop, that he had gone up to talk to them, that Perken had taken a fancy to him, as an ex-soldier, saying that he was a good fellow, and had asked him to join them. He was released on the same day.

So much for the trio. It is now necessary to reconstruct, as best one can, the calendar and the itinerary of what became known to the judicial authorities both sides of the border, and thus to historians of popular habit, assumptions, and leisure, as *l'affaire Perken* (though it could arguably have been called *l'affaire Hofman,* as much a leading spirit as his

tall companion). All three had served from four to six years in the Royal
Dutch Foot Artillery. On 13 July 1808, while stationed at Burghsluis, on
the Isle of Shouwen, they had gone out on a drinking spree, as a result
of which they had decided to desert from their unit, the third company
of the second battalion. We next hear of them in the neighbourhood,
robbing a farm near Renesse, at the northern tip of the island, an operation carried out at night, while armed, and with their faces blackened.
On this occasion, they got away with a little money—enough to pay
for more drink—and with a cheese. We do not know how soon they
were caught, but the operation seems to have been singularly inept, and
they cannot have been free for long. In any case, on 22 June 1809,
nearly a year later, and presumably after a longish period of imprison-
ment, the *juges échevins* of Zierickzee, the principal town on Schouwen,
condemned them to be flogged, branded, and exhibited for a day, after
which they were to be banished from the Kingdom of Holland, a fate
which seems particularly to have depressed Perken. It was presumably
immediately after this that the three had considered their first plan,
which was Hofman's idea : this was to rob, and, in the event of resistance, to kill, an elderly cattle-merchant who had a farm at Poortvliet,
in the centre of the Island of Tholen. Hofman had already been inside
the place, having been billeted there some time previously, while in the
artillery : he had noticed plenty of visible evidence of wealth and
affluence inside the farm. Equally important, the old man and an elderly
female servant had been the only persons to sleep in the house. So it
seemed a promising and relatively easy operation. According to the
summing-up by the prosecution, two years later :

> Ills avaient concerté ensemble de coucher la nuit dans une grange, et, le
> lendemain, de bonne heure, ou bien pendant que les personnes seraient à
> l'église, d'effectuer leurs projets de vol et au besoin d'assassiner.

However, they were to think better of it; for they quickly realised that
the geography of the low-lying island, criss-crossed with waterways
and ditches, and with only rare bridges and raised roads, would force
them back the way that they had come, along a predictable and very
visible route that would be ill-suited to an easy and rapid escape.

> Mais réfléchissant qu'il y avait un quai à passer et où il faudrait repasser,
> ce plan fut rejeté, d'autant qu'il y avait trop à risquer...

It was a wise decision; Tholen might be excellent smuggling country,
thanks to its many inlets, thanks too to the no doubt widespread complicity of the islanders, but its topography was on the contrary extremely
unfavourable to banditry of any kind, especially on the part of strangers.

It was also an island, so that, to reach the mainland, they would have been forced to take one of two ferries, the one at Vogelzung, the other at Tholen. For it was unlikely that three former deserters, all of them strangers to the island, would have had the use of a boat.

The plan on which they fell back was this time Perken's idea. Just as Hofman had had a chance to see the inside of the farm at Poortvliet, Perken had, a little over a year previously, slept at an inn in the hamlet of Notendaal between Kruisland and Blauwe Sluis. He had noticed, on that occasion, that the only people to have slept in the inn—which was also a wineshop and a general store, isolated from any other habitation —were the owners, a couple in their sixties, Laurens Huybregt and his wife, née Elisabeth van Aart, and a young female servant. Perken does not seem to have given much thought to the escape route, for, in this area too, the numerous watercourses would not allow much choice; and, as we shall see, the trio had to ask their way several times before even arriving near the scene of their operations. But Notendaal had in its favour that it was very close to the frontier, and Perken seems to have believed that, once in Brabant with their spoils, they would be safe enough. It would take them little more than half a day to walk out of the Kingdom of Holland, and Perken claimed to know the border area from the coast as far west as Tilburg. And they could not stay where they were :

> Qu'ils ne pouvaient rester chez leurs parents, qu'ils étaient privés de tout, et avaient l'air de déserteurs sans espoir d'améliorer leur sort, que cependant il falloit vivre, boire et manger.

He does not seem to have had any difficulty in convincing the other two of these simple facts of life, as well as of the merits of his plan. He clinched his argument by saying that he had no doubt, from his own observations, that the Huybregt couple were very well-off and that there was a considerable fortune to be made at their expense.

After serving their sentence in Zierickzee, the three men had presumably been given passports to enable them to leave the country; and Perken had decided that they should head for Brabant. But the exact itinerary that they followed in July 1809 is difficult to reconstruct, owing to conflicting evidence. At the time of his arrest in Antwerp, Perken was to claim that he had only set out from Amsterdam on the Friday, 21 July; this would have made it materially impossible for him to have reached the neighbourhood of Rosendaal by the following day. That is no doubt why he stuck so obstinately to his story. But Kroes, who proved more amenable under repeated cross-examination, was eventually to state that they had all gone in the first instance to Dordrecht, and that there they had separated, agreeing to meet again in the town in a couple of days, before heading for Brabant. Kroes had used the interval to look up a relative in Amsterdam, in the hope of borrowing money from him for the journey. Then they had left Dordrecht together, taking a day and a half, in easy stages, from there to Rosendaal. The first night on the road, they had slept in a field outside Breda, near one of the gates of the town, the *Bospoort*, taking care to avoid the town itself. At three on the Friday morning, as soon as the gates were opened, they had gone through the town. By half past four they had reached a village, probably called Lage Banken, where they had stopped at an inn for a drink of *genièvre*. But according to another, perhaps more reliable, source, because it depends on visual testimony, they had been seen at Etten, farther along the road from Breda to Rosendaal, as early as four a.m. They seem to have stayed in the village for most of the day, for they were not seen again till Friday evening, when they were spotted making their way along the raised road known as the *Bugweg*, from Rosendaal to Steenbergen. And we know that they spent Friday night sleeping in hay, in a field known as *Blokkeland*, where a farm worker, who had chosen a similar bed, had noticed them settling down for the night *à la brune*. They were seen very early on the Saturday morning, a little before dawn, that is about three a.m., shaking the hay out of their clothes and hair, by two brothers, already up, and busy loading hay on to a cart. There was an exchange of greetings; and the brothers had shown them the quickest way to reach Steenbergen, along the *Hanen-gevegt*, which was presumably one of the innumerable streams that cut up, in minute rectangles, the watery countryside.

They were next seen at half past three on the Saturday morning, 22 July, when they called for a light for their pipes at the inn near Kruis-land kept by the mother of Angelina Stellmaar. Their pipes lit, they seem to have spent most of the morning walking eastwards, and, apparently without anything to eat. They took care to avoid going through Steenbergen itself because a company of their old regiment was stationed there. Crossing a bridge by an isolated house with a red roof (such was the recollection of Kroes) at about four in the afternoon, they lay down in the corn for a few hours. Kroes would have it that they set off again about seven in the evening; but they were seen by Deneve and his companions at about six, at the Sas or Stoofdijk, walking below the level of the dike. Shortly afterwards, they called at the inn kept by Neyssen's mother, at the *Zevente Ruyte*, leaving the place between half past six and seven, to take the road along the top of the dike to Noten-daal. Perken, who now knew the way from here to the inn at which he had stayed, was seen striding ahead of the other two, walking at speed and with a sense of purpose.

They had reached their destination by eight, for this was the time at which Maria Potters, on her return from the market at Nieuwemolen, had seen them, seated at a table, two of them with their backs against the wall, the third and smaller man facing inwards, drinking beer at Laurens Huybregt's inn, and engaged in an animated conversation with the innkeeper and his wife. They must in fact already have been there for some time, for, an hour earlier, at about seven, the innkeeper's wife had called on the farmer van Hoof, telling his wife that she had three visitors, young fellows, who were going to stay the night, and that she did not very much like the look of them. Van Hoof then thought that he would see for himself—visitors were presumably rather rare in Notendaal, which was well off any main road—and so he called at the inn for a drink at about half past eight. The tallest of the three, after a few tentative *politesses,* asked the farmer point blank if he were going to stay at the inn for the night; van Hoof said that he would be going home, and Perken's affability became almost overwhelming. At about nine, they were seen at the inn by the baker, Mes, and by a young girl in a straw hat who came for a drink unaccompanied. Perken told her that they would be going to bed early, as they had to be on their way early next morning, as they had work to do in Zeeland, where they had already sent on their tools. Mes did not question the probability of starting on a new job on a Sunday. A little later, he was told that they had just come from Tilburg, a distance of thirteen leagues, and that they were tired out. Both van Hoof and Mes were puzzled by the claim made by the tallest of the trio that he had met them on a previous occasion, and that he had lent them a hand with making mead. Neither of them could remember either Perken or having brewed such a beverage, though they were to state much later that they would not have been likely to have forgotten a man of such giant stature and distinguishable from a tattoo design on his arm. While van Hoof, Mes and the girl were still in the inn, the three men asked the innkeeper's wife if she could give them supper, and she told them that she could give them eggs and potatoes, and began peeling the latter. Perken asked her how much they owed for the meal and the drinks, as well as for a night's lodgings, and she replied that she was not in the habit of accepting money in advance, and that they could pay her the following morning, on departure. Perken, for some reason, insisted, however, on paying at least for the drink, there and then. Can he have had a momentary twinge of conscience at the thought of what was to come? A little later, at about ten, she sat down opposite to them for her own meal. It was a friendly and familiar scene. But Hofman, who, unlike the affable and talkative Perken, seems to have had a distinctly macabre sense of humour, was to recall that, watching her eat her supper with every sign of appetite, he had reflected that this would be the last meal that she would ever take on earth.

Between eleven and eleven-thirty, two farm-workers who were employed on the same farm and who were looking for a pile of hay in which to spend the night, passed by the inn. By the light coming from the half-open door, they could see and recognise the innkeeper's wife outside, closing the shutters, and they greeted her good evening, but she apparently did not hear them, going inside without a word, and locking the door behind her. At about the same time, they heard a noise coming from the interior; and one of them said to the other that it sounded as if a chair had been overturned. They thought no more about it, leaving the top of the dike to climb down to the level of the field. They must have just missed Perken, who, at much the same time, had had the beginnings of a nose bleed, and had gone outside, waiting for it to stop. It can hardly have been a signal to the other two; for noses do not bleed to order. But Hofman saw this opportunity and came outside to join Perken, and the two held a sort of counsel of war. Perken was for strangling the elderly couple—the visitors van Hoof, Mes and the girl had gone off after ten—while Hofman thought it would be more expeditious to cut their throats. Kroes seems to have remained inside during this conversation, though Perken later asserted that he had had a word with him a little earlier, when they had both asked their hostess the way to the lavatory.[1]

The two farm-workers must have narrowly missed being witnesses to the murder. Indeed, the sound of the chair being upset was probably the actual attack on Laurens Huybregt, in the ground-floor room. For, according to the vital testimony of Hofman, it was at about eleven-thirty that Elisabeth van Aart had told them it was time they all went to bed, as they all had to be up early on the Sunday morning. He had followed her upstairs, where she had shown them the room and the bed in which the three of them were to sleep. As she was preparing to leave, Hofman tried to induce her to carry on the conversation a little longer, but she insisted that it was time for bed. He caught her from behind and slit her throat with a jack-knife. She did, however have time to scream, for the two men down below heard her death cry: *O Jesus,*

---

[1] Kroes gives the following version, when questioned on 20 September 1809: '. . . . il se rendit aux cabinets où il fut rejoint par les autres qui lui dirent, *Jean, viens, il y a fortune à faire ici cette nuit*; il ne voulait rien entendre, disant qu'il était déjà assez malheureux d'avoir été contraint à quitter sa patrie, il est donc parti seul sur un chemin, passant la nuit dans un bois où, le matin, il fut rejoint par les deux autres, portant un paquet noué dans un mouchoir rouge, le partage fut fait dans un bois, les deux lui dirent qu'ils avaient tué les vieux.' Kroes stuck to this improbable version for some time, but eventually admitted that he had been in the inn, downstairs, at the time of the murders.

Maria. This was the signal for them to set on an astonished Huybregt, Kroes tipping him up from behind, while Perken cut his throat with Hofman's knife.[1] Hofman then suggested that as both their hosts were dead, it was now time to think about having a proper meal; and after looking around the kitchen, they took three bottles of wine and some ham. Having put these aside, they searched the house and found either sixty or six hundred florins, in gold pieces, under the couple's bed, a number of coloured neckerchiefs, a little jewellery and a watch. Hofman removed the rings from the woman's fingers, as well as her ear-rings and the silver buckles from her shoes. After a last look round, they let themselves out by the back door, taking the wine and food with them. Kroes at first was to insist that he had already left before the murders, and that the other two had met him at a pre-arranged spot in a wood some time in the early hours.[2] But his interrogators were quick to point out that, not knowing the area—as he had never been there before—he could hardly have been in a position to agree on a rendezvous, and he eventually admitted that he had been present at the whole operation. Having left the inn, they shared out the booty, which was meagre enough, in a small wood. Hofman got two neckerchiefs, one red, the other white— he was wearing one, bearing the embroidered laundry mark 'L3 III', which the wife of van Hoof, who had done the washing for the old couple, identified as being that of Laurens Huybregt, at the time of his arrest. Kroes was given some jewellery, neckerchief, the shoe buckles and about twenty florins. Perken presumably kept the rest as his part. They then sat down in a field of colza and drank one of the bottles of wine, throwing the other two into a watercourse, after which they set out in the night, at about three in the morning, towards the border.

They reached the frontier at Essen at about eight on the Sunday morning; first of all they reported to the *commissaire de police* to have their passports checked; these were in their own names. Then Perken and Hofman attended mass at the village church, singing a *requiem* for

---

[1] Questioned on 8 January 1810, Kroes stated: '. . . lequel des 3 fut le premier assaillant. Répond que Hofman fut le premier assaillant, qu'il avait demandé à la femme de lui montrer le lit où il devait coucher, que la femme voulut le lui montrer, et qu'étant entrés ensemble elle et lui dans la chambre, la femme fut attaquée par Hofman, qu'elle voulut se défendre, et saisit Hofman à la poitrine, que lui déposant entendit la femme s'écrier *O Jésus Maria!* que Hofman lui coupa le cou ou la gorge avec un couteau pliant, que tandis que la femme fut assaillie par Hofman, Perken saisit l'homme à la gorge, et le serra au point de l'empêcher de rendre aucun son.' But on the 12th Perken incriminated Kroes more directly: '. . . que lui déposant entendit la femme faire un cri et a cru entendre qu'elle disait *ô! mon bon Jésus! Maria!* que sur ce cri, Jan Croes se leva et poussa Laurens Huybregt par derrière de dessus le banc . . . qu'il tomba par terre, que sur ce Laurens Huybregt s'écria *qu'est-ce? ô hommes! qu'est-ce?*'

[2] See p. 63, n. 1.

the souls of their two victims—a performance which they were to repeat a few days later in an Antwerp church. While the two Catholics were thus engaged in putting their consciences in order, Kroes, who was a Protestant, waited outside the church, using the interval to wipe the front of his shirt, which was stained with blood, in some mud, in an attempt to make the stains less visible.[1] Later he was to explain the presence of the blood by the fact that not only Perken, but he too had had a nose bleed the night before.[2] After the others had come out of mass, the three went to the local inn, played cards, drank some beer and ate some soup. They appeared to be in excellent humour, and they spent freely.

According to Jannssens, the Belgian arrested with two of them a few days later, they then headed straight for Antwerp, for Jannssens was convinced that he had met them in an inn called *le Pavillon français*—later he gave its name as *le Drapeau danois*—on the Borgenhout, a favourite gathering place for the inhabitants of the port: workmen, lovers, artisans and shop-keepers, on their days off. As the Borgenhout was very much a Sunday rendezvous, Jannssens seems to have convinced himself that he had first met the trio on a Sunday afternoon, when the promenades and its many noisy inns would have been particularly crowded. He had been sitting in the inn when the three had come in; Jannssens, who had served in the Dutch army, at once recognised them as Dutchmen, and introduced himself to Perken, who seemed to be the leader, in that language. Perken, with his usual rather boisterous affability, clapped him on the shoulder, saying that he seemed to be a good fellow, and inviting him to sit at their table and have a drink with them. He seems to have had several, for not only did the four spend the rest of the day together, being joined at one stage by some prostitutes, but they had supper together, and Jannssens remained with Kroes and Perken up to the time of their arrest. But, in his testimony, he seems to have put his meeting with the trio three days too early. What he thought

---

[1] '... les deux autres sont allés à la messe, lui, étant de la religion réformée, n'y est pas allé, puis ils ont bu à l'auberge' (Kroes, 20 September 1809). '... Que le dimanche du 23 ... Cornelis Perken et Christian Hofman y assistèrent [à Essen] au service catholique romain, et qu'à cette occasion ils firent dire une messe de requiem pour les âmes de Laurens Huybregt et Elisabeth van Aart qu'ils avaient assassiné, et adorèrent le Dieu Tout Puissant ! ! !... ils étaient convenus ensemble que lorsqu'ils seraient arrivés à Anvers de faire dire des messes de requiem pour les personnes par eux assassinées et qu'ils destinaient pour cela 4 escalins, et qu'ils se souviendraient d'elles dans leurs prières' (the case for the prosecution, 17 January 1810). Rather surprisingly, the prosecutor seems to have found this concern for the souls of their victims on the part of Perken and Hofman either scandalous or impudent. But there seems little doubt that they were in fact perfectly sincere.

[2] Later, he was to claim to have had one in Wuustwezel, the day after the crime, and that this was how the front of his shirt had been stained with blood.

had happened on the Sunday almost certainly occurred on the Wednesday.

For, according both to Hofman and to a female servant from an inn at Wuustwezel, to whom they gave their shirts to be washed and ironed, after leaving Essen they had walked to this village, eating there in the evening, playing cards, and spending the night there three in one bed. This is certainly a more credible itinerary in view of the fact that they had not left Essen till about two or three in the afternoon. On the following day, Monday, they passed through Hoogstraten, possibly to look up a local goldsmith known to Hofman (who may have been anxious to dispose of some of the objects stolen from the murdered couple, or who may merely have been seeking work, as he was to say at his trial) and spent the night of Monday to Tuesday, 24-5 July, at an inn in Merksplas, again three to a bed. But at least, after the visit to Notendaal, they could allow themselves this relative luxury, rather than sleep in the hay. From Merksplas, they turned south to Westmalle—they seem to have been anxious to skirt Turnhout—then kept on the road to Antwerp as far as St Antonius, where they stopped off at an inn for the night of Tuesday to Wednesday. This would have got them at last to Antwerp on the morning of Wednesday 26 July. After leaving Notendaal, they had moved in a wide circle to the north-east of Antwerp, no doubt assuming that once the murder had been discovered and the hue and cry raised, the Dutch authorities would have assumed that the three would have taken the most direct route to the Flemish port.

It was presumably some time on the Wednesday that they met Jannssens at the Borgenhout. The four spent the Wednesday night at an inn called *le Cygne*. The next day, Hofman decided to part company with his companions, in order to make a second attempt to contact the goldsmith at Hoogstraten. Friday seems to have been an exceptionally good day for the three travellers. They had been to a pawnshop in the suitably named rue des Vertus in the morning, leaving behind the victim's watch. They had spent the rest of the day drinking, picking up some women, to whom they proposed an excursion *à six* to the Borgenhout, but the women said they would rather go on drinking in the city, so they settled down at an inn called *la Vigne*. It was on leaving this place late in the evening, without the women, and in the intention of returning to *le Cygne* (where bloodstained linen and wide sailors' trousers were discovered in their room), that Perken, Kroes and the unfortunate Jannssens, who must have cursed his luck of the previous two days, were arrested, place Verte, 'near the cemetery', and brought before the *commissaire de police de la première Section* who, after questioning them in Flemish (at this level of repressive personnel, local officials were generally natives, though the public prosecutor, Piorry, was a French-

man, an ex-Conventionnel and a regicide[1]), turned them in at the *Amigo*
—and there would have been no difficulty in establishing the identity of
the two Dutchmen, as they were travelling under valid passports
delivered to them by the authorities of Zierickzee, and under their own
names (with slight alterations in the case of Perken and with deliberately
deceptive destinations, for there is nothing to suggest that any of them
was intending to go to Turnhout, which was given as their eventual
destination). That, as far as the two were concerned, was the end of
their trip, which had lasted only six days, though they were all to do
the return journey, this time by a much more direct route. Hofman
seems to have been arrested the next day, Saturday 29 July, at Westmalle, on his way to Hoogstraten, just a week after the murders.

There seems to have been no rhyme or reason in the semi-circular
itinerary that they had adopted, other than the need to avoid, whenever
possible, entering towns, going through the gates of cities; it was much
more as if the itinerary was dictated to them by the roads themselves.
Perhaps it was the vague awareness of the fragility of their present existence on the roads with money for once in their pockets that had induced
these rather bewildered men to throw themselves, with an almost febrile
energy, into a constant round of pleasure, of eating and drinking, playing
cards, talking to strangers, entertaining *filles de joie*, boasting of their
various skills (Kroes, for instance, was at one time claiming to be a
brewer, at another, he declared that he had been trained as a tailor)
reminiscing about life in an army from which they had but recently
deserted, a round of pleasure interrupted only by the various, generally
comfortably short stretches of their roundabout walk. It was not as if
they appeared to be in any great hurry even to put as much distance as
possible between themselves and the scene of their crime. The likelihood
of finding a privateer just at the right time and in the right place must
have seemed fairly remote, if they were ever sober enough to give the
matter serious thought. And it could hardly be said that Antwerp was
in the centre of a distant and foreign land. There was a constant coming
and going over the frontier, which was so close both in physical and in
mental terms, and which, even to these simple and sanguine men, must
have appeared to offer only a derisory wall of protection. So the best
thing to do would be to pack in as much pleasure, as much food and
drink, as much experience, as if to tide them over a lifetime. The two
Catholics had, after all, cleared their consciences on the Sunday morning,
and could then devote themselves to enjoyment and to the easy sociability
of sailors' inns in a great port. We do not know how Kroes stood with

---

[1] See my *Paris and its Provinces, op. cit.,* p. 254. Piorry greatly disliked the
Antwerpers, claiming that they had always defied authority, that they were smugglers
to a man, and that they disdained the benefits of French rule.

his conscience, though he seems to have been less concerned with absolution, salvation and forgiveness than his companions.[1] When dealing with people who were clearly very stupid, it is almost impossible to reconstruct the mental processes that may have dictated their itinerary, their public behaviour, and their conduct. Of the latter, all that one can say with any degree of conviction would be that, following their condemnation by the Zierickzee court and their banishment from the Kingdom of Holland, they had to do *something*, and do it very quickly : for them it was a matter of life and death. At Notendaal, they opted for the easiest, most obvious solution to their immediate difficulties; for a couple of elderly people living alone in an inn would be the easiest of all targets in eighteenth- and early nineteenth-century conditions. There would not even be the initial problem of breaking-in. The rest would follow from that single decision. For Perken and Kroes, who had decided at some stage that their best eventual course would be to find a privateer that would be ready to take them on, without too many questions being asked, the cathedral quarter of Antwerp would have been the obvious place to have gone. We know from other sources that the Borgenhout was a favourite meeting place for smugglers and for all those who, for one reason or another, were concerned to conduct their business, presumably illegitimate, outside the city walls, and well away from the attention of police spies; and it is likely that *le Pavillon français,* or *le Drapeau danois,* had a naval rather than a Chinese connotation, and that such a place would be likely to be frequented by sailors. Kroes and Perken had a vague idea as to what sort of place they were looking for. Hofman, on the other hand, who does not seem to have had *le pied marin,* had no reason to stay on in the city, once he had exhausted the round of pleasure. But he was brought back there on Sunday 30 July, and was questioned by the *commissaire* on the following day. On the Monday evening, all four were once more together in the *Amigo.* But on Tuesday 1 August the *commissaire* ordered the release of their fortuitous companion, Jannssens, and this is the last we hear of the former *enfant de troupe.* It is possible that his release may have been a reward for having brought the police on to the tracks of the other two; for he does seem to have shown considerable eagerness to gain their friendship. Or it may have been simply that the *commissaire* had decided that he was telling the truth.

Meanwhile, in Notendaal, the judicial process had been set in motion, very early on the Sunday morning, 23 July, with the discovery of the

---

[1] 'Article 66. On lui demande s'il ne reconnaît donc pas que, quelque coupable que soit un homme, le salut de son âme est le seul but qu'il doit se proposer, quand bien même tout espoir serait perdu pour lui sur la terre? Répond, Oui ...' (Kroes, 20 September 1809).

shoeless bodies of the innkeeper and his wife, the former downstairs, in the main room, the latter in the guest room. The bodies seem to have been discovered by van Hoof or by his wife, who had noticed that the shutters were still closed; both had been alarmed by the appearance and the behaviour of the three strangers. And, in this part of the world, peasants were up with the dawn, even on a Sunday morning. As there were no police in a hamlet like Notendaal, the authorities of Steenbergen were presumably contacted. In any case, it was the *bailli* of Steenbergen and his assistants who began taking statements from Boeyers, Mes, and van Hoof, the last people to have seen the couple alive. Neyssen, Marie Potters and Deneve followed on Tuesday 25 July; and the authorities received further statements on 10, 25 and 27 September, 11 and 16 October, and 5 November. Kroes was cross-examined repeatedly, until, on 8 January 1810, he finally abandoned his ridiculous story about having spent the night of the murder in a wood, meeting his two companions a little before dawn, and then being told what had happened, and admitted to having been present at the inn at the time of the crime, though, even then, he denied ever having been anything more than a witness to the murder of Laurens Huybregt. He was a remarkably stupid and obstinate young man; and his questioners do not seem to have been able to impress him as much as the other two with the enormity of their act and with the terror of divine retribution. He was a Protestant, but, after all, according to his own admission, not a very zealous one. He had never received regular instruction from the *dominies.* Perken was cross-examined on 19 September and on 12 January. His questioners had little trouble with him. He readily admitted everything, was talkative, helpful, and boastful; his main concern seems to have been to impress his judges that he had been the master-mind behind the whole operation. Hofman proved far more recalcitrant, and he had to be closely questioned on 19, 22 and 23 September, 11 and 16 November, and 2 December, before he finally admitted having killed Elisabeth van Aart. The case for the prosecution was put on 17 January 1810; on 15 February the court condemned the three young men to death by hanging. The next day, Hofman and Perken both asked to make statements, the former on the subject of his correct age, the latter, on that of his Christian name and birthplace. All three expressed extreme contrition, and refused appeal, 'suppliant les juges d'avoir égard à leur grande jeunesse, témoignant être pénétrés du plus profond repentir de leurs forfaits, demandant en outre qu'on leur accordât des pasteurs ou prêtres, chacun suivant sa religion'.

On Wednesday 28 February, they were executed in front of the town hall of Steenbergen, Kroes first, Perken second and Hofman last. Thus, in death, Perken had been denied the leading rôle that he had so insistently assumed for himself from the moment that the three had deserted from their regiment. Hofman had this thrust upon him presumably as the cruel murderer of the woman who had treated them with trust and friendliness and had readily made food for them. The judges clearly felt, and said so on a number of occasions, that this acceptance of hospitality greatly added to the enormity of the crime. So it was over Hofman's head that, on the orders of the judges, the murder weapon, described as *un couteau pliant*, was displayed on the day of execution. And over the head of each of the three was placed a notice in large letters, on a wooden board : MEURTRIER DE DEUX PERSONNES. The bodies were to remain hanging for the rest of the day, till nightfall.

As an account of a sordid, brutal and disgusting crime, *l'affaire Perken* is of little interest to the historian. It was in no way an unusual crime, innkeepers in isolated places offering ready victims to those in desperate need of food and money. In this respect, it was a typical product of poverty and extreme need, though the perpetrators did not deny themselves the usual fringe benefits of raiding the cellar and of going off with objects that, in their opinion, would contribute to their elegance, a preoccupation that seems very much to have been in their minds. Even Kroes, or perhaps especially Kroes, was anxious to make the best of himself. Perken seems to have walked with a sailor's swagger, and Hofman was much concerned to show his face to advantage above a neatly-tied white or red stock. Such preoccupation might seem somewhat infantile, but these were very simple, crude men, illiterate or barely literate, whose only wealth was the good looks, the long limbs, and the physical stamina that God had given them. Equally characteristic is their stupidity, both in the manner in which they conducted their terrible operation, and in their behaviour after it had been committed. These were not cunning professionals, but desperate and thoughtless young men. There seems to have been little doubt that they were terribly frightened by what they had done, and that what they dreaded most was divine retribution. Their judges played on these fears to great effect.

It is not then as individuals and as cruel murderers that they need detain us any longer. But *l'affaire Perken* is of interest in a much wider context, for, like the various angles of a prism, it reflects social assumptions on a number of related matters : the sociability and the affability of the walking traveller, popular humour, the working hours and the sleeping habits of the very poor, the extent to which itineraries can be dictated by a predictable topography, the avoidance of towns, the relative safety of places *extra-muros*, beyond the gates, for those in trouble or merely for those, so numerous in a border area, anxious to avoid awkward encounters with authority, the lusty, almost febrile, amusements of the very poor at leisure, their places of entertainment, the simple, again predictable, itineraries of drink and pleasure, the somewhat macabre element of accident, the importance of laundrywomen or female servants as an evident source of detection. This particular double murder could no doubt witness for scores of similar murders, whether in Holland or in France, in most of these respects. But two important elements certainly particularise it from the average run of internal and accasional crime : the one is the proximity to the frontier, the other, the very landscape, a landscape that makes recognition so easy, and escape so difficult. It is indeed hard to hide in an area criss-crossed with dikes, polders, and small bridges. Everywhere the three men went, in the course of their round-about journey, they must have been seen, and commented upon, by scores of people in full daylight, at dawn, at dusk, or even in the dead of night.

There are plenty of examples, in the evidence submitted to the French *Grand Juge,* of the picaresque politeness of a walking world, and of the readiness to engage in conversation of the moving population of inns, posting-houses, sailors' cabarets and public promenades. Anthony Luistenburg, one of two brothers, engaged a little before dawn in load-ing hay on to their cart, sees the three men getting out of their bed of hay in a field, greeting them :

> ... *mes camarades, vous avez eu un bon logement cette nuit,* sur quoi ils respon-dirent, *oui, notre bourgeois* [they must have recognised in the brothers, not mere day labourers, but affluent farmers], *la soirée nous avait surpris et nous ne pumes aller plus loin,* et que les 3 inconnus causant sur la route avec le déposant lui firent connaître qu'ils voulaient suivre le long de la métairie de Gabriel.

One of the farm-labourers, as he passes the inn between eleven and eleven-thirty on the evening of the murder, greets Huybregt's wife *bonsoir, voisine,* and is surprised when she does not reply. The woman herself tells the travellers : *'C'est bien, mes enfants, j'apprêterai des pommes de terre avec des oeufs . . .'* and, a little later, with the same easy familiarity, she informs the young men : *'Allons, mes enfants, je vais vous montrer où vous allez coucher'*; and, just before killing her, Hofman asks her : *'Comment, la mère—vous vous retirez déjà . . .?'* There is rather a macabre exchange between Perken and the innkeeper, on the arrival of the three at Notendaal : *'. . . eh bien, notre maître, vous vivez donc encore?* sur quoi Huybregt répondit *mais oui da, mon garçon, j'espère même encore vivre longtems, car cela dure trop longtems d'être mort.'* It was an appropriately worded *entrée en matière,* a sort of un-conscious bravado on the part of the poor man, to an evening which would result in his murder. And equally appropriate, as an example of insensitivity, is Hofman's alleged proposal, just after the two murders had been committed; *maintenant nous allons [nous] soigner pour la bouffaille*, though this too may have contained an element of bravado or have been designed to reassure himself or the others. Jannssen describes his first encounter with the three, in the inn off the Borgenhout outside Antwerp :

> ... que s'étant aperçu qu'ils étoient hollandois, il leur avoit parlé dans cette langue, en leur faisant entendre qu'il avait servi en Hollande, qu'alors le plus grand des deux dit qu'il voyoit qu'il étoit bon garçon, l'invita de boire avec eux, qu'ayant bu la goutte ensemble, le même lui avait dit qu'il devait toucher 500 florins ce jour-là en le priant de l'accompagner ... il est allé avec lui à son auberge *au Cygne* où ils ont trouvé son compagnon et où il a dîné avec eux sur leur invitation, qu'après le dîner étant retournés au cabaret *le Drapeau danois* ils y ont trouvé 2 femmes avec lesquelles ils se sont proposés d'aller promener à Borgerhout, que ces femmes ayant témoigné le désir d'aller plutôt au cabaret appellé *la Vigne* dans la rue des Juifs, ils se rendaient dans ce cabaret...

The conversation and the rather confused itinerary of a day spent drinking are both engagingly familiar; they recall the language and the rapid cascade of events and of moves in *Gil Blas*, and we encounter the same readiness to inform and to inquire in any judicial document of the late eighteenth century that reflects on the habits and the speech of the itinerant population of France. Perken, for instance, seems genuinely disappointed when Huybregt tells him that he cannot remember him, that, indeed, it would be difficult for an innkeeper to recall all the faces that had passed through his house; the tall young man evidently believed that the sight of him should have been quite unforgettable. He made a similar ploy to van Hoof. The first part was clearly dictated by practical considerations, but the latter seems to have been purely conversational and to have been inspired by the same insistent desire to be remembered, as if he was trying to gain at least honorary admission even into this rather sad, hard-working and frugal rural community. Perken was after all himself of peasant origin, and, because he had not seen his parents for some time, he may have tried to see in the inmates of Huybregt's inn his *pays* (and all three expressed genuine distress at the prospect of the exile that had been imposed upon them) :

> que l'un des 3 ... le plus grand, lui dit *Van Hoof, restez-vous coucher ici?* sur quoi il répondit *Non,* ajoutant, *je demeure près d'ici, mais il paraît que vous me connaisse?* sur quoi l'inconnu répondit *ne vous connaîtrais-je pas? J'ai travaillé ici à la composition de l'hydromel dont vous êtes un des intéressés, et vous êtes trouvé souvent présent aux travaux,* que cependant le déposant ne put se rappeller l'avoir vu souvent.

In view of what he had come to do at the inn, it is difficult to see why

Perken should have been so desperately anxious, as it were, to establish
an identity with these people, who regarded him as a stranger. It would
have appeared on the contrary to have been elementary common-sense
to have revealed as little as possible, both about himself and about his
companions. Yet here is the big fool utterly insistent to have these people
say that, after an absence of a year or two, they could still remember
him. He even includes Laurens Huybregt, his chosen victim, in this
strange circle of recalled acquaintanceship. Of course, he may have been
trying to reassure the other customers, as well as the old couple, by
insisting that he was not in fact a total stranger, that he had been this
way before, and he was obviously trying to sound out van Hoof as to
where he was going to sleep (if he had said : at the inn, he would either
have been signing his own death warrant, or the operation would no
doubt have been called off). It does, however, seem much more likely
that, on the eve of what, even if everything went exactly according to
plan, was likely to be a very long exile indeed—none of the three could
expect to be able to return to their native Holland perhaps for twenty
years at least, after which they might expect an amnesty—Perken and
his companions were anxious to establish themselves, as human beings,
as social persons, with the last group of compatriots that they were likely
to be seeing for many years ahead. To these young men, France was an
unknown country, and though they no doubt could understand it,
Flemish would still be a foreign language. Although they were deserters,
they were even anxious to let Mes, van Hoof and the others, anyone in
fact who would listen to them, know that they had been in the Dutch
army : another argument in favour of recognition, another plea for
acceptance as members of a community, another, rather pathetic cry
to be released from loneliness : the vaguely idiotic pride in an army that
they had rejected, from which they had deserted, but the values of which
they were attempting to retain. We are not dealing with educated people
who express themselves with care. And when faced with material of this
kind, it is incumbent on the historian to force as much hidden meaning
as his imagination or his experience will allow him out of every sentence
of reported speech. It is as much a calculation of probabilities as a study
of realities. Behind the conventional greetings, the boisterous humour,
and the easy-going affability of travellers, there lies a whole tentative
world of assumptions that can sometimes be hinted at. Greetings are
groping signals of mutual recognition, conversation, on general and
everyday themes, inn small talk, are the first, timid steps in a ballet
involving participants who have many reasons to be afraid of one another,
to suspect one another's motives. To offer information about oneself,
one's recent itinerary, one's destination is a means calculated to lower

defences and to lessen suspicions. Perken, Hofman and Kroes were young men who had lost their way in more ways than one.

So this is not merely the record of a double murder, as preserved in the formal language of the law—all the more formal for having been further filtered through the medium of translation into French : for all the conversations that we have quoted were of course spoken in Dutch. The considerable amount of evidence presented by a dossier that fills a single box enables the attentive observer to make a brief, yet evocative journey—even the colour of the roof of a farmhouse, the straw hat on a girl's head are sketched in *en passant*—into the early nineteenth-century world of the very poor and the very laborious. It is as far removed as the Russian steppe from the elegant and comfort-loving existence of the patrician classes of Amsterdam or The Hague. We are among the gnarled bovine faces and under the windswept, ominous skies of van Gogh's potato pickers, though in this summer scene there is more light and plenty of colour. Here is a society many members of which will habitually sleep out in the open during the summer months, and who will consider themselves lucky to be allowed a corner in a barn during the winter ones. Perken, Kroes and Hofman, even when they have money to pay for a room in an inn—a rare and much-appreciated luxury—will sleep all three to a bed, probably because they had always done so, would not even have thought of doing otherwise. And perhaps, too, now that they were bound together by the common fact of desertion and associated in a common crime, they felt even greater need for each other's company. There was at least a residual strength in the existence of the trio.

These are people too for whom every article of clothing represents a precious capital, as well as a manifestation of pride; and we can sense the satisfaction of Hofman when, looking into a mirror in one of the Brabant inns, he carefully ties his red neckerchief under his chin; and, even when they are on the run—an expression purely metaphorical for people who, once they have the frontier behind them, dawdle, without any apparent sense of purpose or urgency, as if they were attempting to kill time, waiting for they did not know just what—apart from food, drink and sleep, their thought is above all for clothes, not so much as a disguise, not in order to alter their appearance, but to make them feel better, to embellish them, perhaps too to make the future seem less menacing : for who, as it were under sentence of death, would think of having a jacket and a waistcoat made—and this can be done on the spot, in a matter of hours—or purchase three new round hats? Yet this is what they do, on one of their stops.

Through their vision, or that of those whom they meet in rural inns or in sailors' dives, we can glimpse the easy, thoughtless generosity of the poor, the ability to sacrifice even the next day for the next hour, the inquiry as to the location of the nearest pawnshop, nicknamed in this part of the world *un lombard* (as evocative as the local expression for prison, *l'amigo*), the wide-sweeping gesture—'drink with us', 'sup with us', 'stay with us', 'pick up girls with us'—a brief fastidious entry into the magic world of aristocratic values; and we can follow, perhaps better than they could themselves, in the befuddled condition provoked by glass after glass of *genièvre,* an itinerary of wineshops, cabarets and inns only explainable in terms of the tortured topography of the Bloed Straat, of the labyrinth of streets winding in on themselves in the old port quarter of Antwerp. We can appreciate, too, through the eyes of Perken, who has walked thirteen leagues in a couple of days. the cool luxury of the interior of a whitewashed walled inn and the immense promise of a meal consisting of eggs and potatoes.

We can sense the ill-temper, the mutual accusations. the recriminations of the three, uncertain which way to take next or which was the direction of the frontier; and we can sense the denunciation of Kroes, as he lags behind, by his more stalwart companions. For these people are not walking for pleasure. Who indeed, at this level of society, has ever walked for pleasure? And they are not on a pleasure trip *à la Jean-Jacques.* If they even *notice* the colour of things : the red roof that recurs so frequently in their statements, a line of poplars, a field of colza, a haystack, a small bridge, a quay, the steeple of a church seen from afar in these flat lands, if they even notice and retain these things it is merely as signposts, recognition points, to be retained in case they should have to retrace their steps (as they frequently have to in this waterlogged land-scape). The inn-signs naturally call out to them, full of promise—at least *after* Notendaal, for, *before* Notendaal, they would merely be irritants, temptations best resisted, but they cannot remember the colour of the flag : at one moment it is the Danish one, at another the French tricolor.

We can sense their uneasiness, the feeling that all eyes must be upon them, that they are visibly different, each time that they go into an inn or a wineshop, once on the south side of the frontier; and so we can appreciate their gratitude to Jannssens for having spoken to them, for having provided them with conversation, the main entertainment of the very poor, especially of poor fishermen, seamen, bargees, and carters. And we can even sense their pride in an army that they have betrayed. They were after all still Dutchmen, though cast out from the kingdom; and they had served long enough in the army to have acquired the old, simple, military standards of boastfulness and physical courage.

So this is not a crime story, nor the minute chronicle of a long, and very confused, walk, at a period when most people thought of travel only in terms of a day's walk, a week's walk, or even a month's walk. It is a brief vision of a shared experience : that of an illusory sense of freedom, of almost limitless wealth, of a week or thereabouts in the young lives of three Dutchmen, the combined ages of all three hardly amounting to three score years and ten, a week dominated by a frenetic round of pleasure, by hearty conversation to scotch loneliness, doubt and unnamed fears, by the need to drink in order to attain the safety of sleep and to dim the awful, gnawing sense of guilt—if one *requiem* did not do the trick, then the remedy had to be applied again, and even Kroes seems eventually to have succumbed to religious awe—a trip abroad, almost a fantasy, as time moved faster and faster, all at once to run out, for two of them, Place Verte, near the cemetery, for the third, on the road, in or near Westmalle. A week, in such very young lives, is a very long time indeed. And most of the time that remained to them to live was used to find out all that there was to be found out about that week, all at least that could be expressed, put into words, by people who had few words. We have tried to go one better than the judges, whose curiosity did not go beyond the point of obtaining a conviction and of wresting from the three poor wretches a plea of absolution, and to attempt to reconstruct thoughts and sensations that could not be put into words. The historian has much the same assignment as Proust, but he does not have the advantage of Proust's own memory; he has to construct, then to pillage, other people's. So much then for Perken, Hofman and Kroes, in that order, somehow a juster one than that of their hanging.

PART III

A View on the Street:

Seduction and Pregnancy

in Revolutionary Lyon

A View on the Street

Les diamans, les bijous, un ameublement superbe, un carrosse du dernier goût, tout cela est prêt: un mot, & une bourse de mille louis va précéder.
(Restif de la Bretonne, *La Paysanne pervertie*)

Le jeune Page hardi comme un Page, en vérité! & il n'y a rien de solide là-dedans: ça est trop-jeune, & ça n'a pas d'état, ça sera un fréluquet, qui laisserait là une Femme un-jour, pour aller courir de garnison en garnison, commes les Officiers des cazernes de Joigni, & d'ailleurs.
(Restif, *Monsieur Nicolas*)

... si vous n'avez Personne, je suis bein-sûr de vous faire un-jour Comtesse. Le malheur, c'est que je n'ai que 16 ans! mais je suis orfelin, & les droits des Tuteurs cessent plutôt [sic] que ceux des Pères.
(Restif, *La Paysanne pervertie*)

Pour plaire à la fille
qui est si gentille
c'est à la maman
qu'il faut faire le baratin.
(Parisian rhyme, **XX**th century)

Dans toutes ses visites Pierre Dusurgey fit à la remontrante des promesses de mariage, auxquelles elle crut d'autant plus facilement qu'il n'y avait aucune disproportion dans leurs professions et leurs âges, la remontrante est âgée de 23 ans, et Pierre Dusurgey, de 24; l'un et l'autre travaillaient pour la chapellerie ... il avait pour elle des complaisances marquées; chaque jour, après la journée de travail, il venait la chercher, pour l'accompagner à la promenade, il en faisait autant les fêtes et dimanches, enfin il disait publiquement et à leurs connaissances mutuelles qu'il la recherchait en mariage. (Déclaration de grossesse faite par Benoîte Bonnard, coupeuse de poils pour la chapellerie, devant le tribunal de Lyon-Ville 15 February 1791, Archives départementales du Rhône, 36 L 52)

... Il y a environ un an elle fit la connoissance du Sr. Jaivry, voyageur de commerce pour cette ville à Bordeaux, et habitant alternativement dans l'une ou l'autre de ces deux villes... il lui fit des propositions de mariage, il n'attendait, disait-il, que le moment où il aurait pu parvenir à arranger des affaires de manière à pouvoir se fixer absolument à Lyon. Le Sieur Jaivry se ménageait de tems à autre des entrevues avec la comparante à l'insu de ses parents, il l'entretenait du BONHEUR qu'il disait se promettre du mariage qu'il contracterait *incessamment* avec elle. (Déclaration de grossesse faite par Annette Dementhon, fille du Sr. Dementhon, marchand de dorures fausses, demeurant à Lyon, rue Saint-Dominique, âgée de 17 ans, 21 April 1791)

Dlle. Jeanne Planet, ouvrière en soie, demeurant à Lyon chez Monsieur son père, rue Bourgchanin, fille mineure... qu'il y a environ un an qu'elle fit la connaissance du Sr. François Nicq, serrurier à Lyon... rue Désirée; que ce dernier, charmé de la conduite de la remontrante, *demanda à ses père et mère l'entrée de la maison* et promit d'épouser leur fille. Les père et mère... furent d'autant plus faciles à croire cette promesse que le Sr. Nicq, sans père ni mère, peut disposer de lui et est absolument libre, il venoit donc assidument chez eux. (Déclaration de grossesse faite par Jeanne Planet, ouvrière en soie, 25 May 1791)

Le Sr. Brigand... s'est fait un jeu de tromper son innocence, *peu accoutumée au séjour de la ville*, le Sr. Brigand a profité de son inexpérience et de sa crédulité, et lui a fait entrevoir l'avenir le plus heureux si elle se livrait à lui. (Déclaration de grossesse faite par Pierrette Blanc, brodeuse, Petite rue Tramassac, âgée de 21 ans)

... depuis plus d'une année le Sr. Bavet venait la voir assidument dans son domicile où elle demeuroit alors, allée des Images, *il entretenait même avec elle une correspondance lorsqu'il était absent*, ou que ses moments ne lui permettaient pas de se rendre auprès d'elle. (Déclaration de grossesse faite par Françoise Dueure, brodeuse, quai de Saône, 28 June 1791)

The arguments, like the promised rewards, may vary, but the *langage du coeur*, however phrased, seeks always the same capitulation, and the extracts quoted above spell out, in varied forms, the same sad, sad story. Restif clearly has in mind seduction at a high, or at least, an ascending, social level, and diamonds, jewels, magnificent furniture, a carriage in the very latest style, even a purse containing a thousand *louis* are hardly inducements that will speak to the tender heart of the Lyon *brodeuse* or *ouvrière en soie*, her feet relatively firmly on the ground. For her such promises would appear so improbable as totally to undermine the credibility of the persuader, of what in Parisian cynical parlance would be described as *le baratineur*. It would be necessary to adjust language to the economic expectations and the strongly held social conventions of the addressee. For the working girl, a similar, or very slightly superior economic status would act as a powerful argument. The facts of neigh-bourhood would likewise count, as would old acquaintance, which would appear as a sort of guarantee. The receipt of a letter, or of several letters, proudly displayed to workmates, and no doubt read out loud by one of them, would be much more convincing than a purse of gold. A man without parents would hold a powerful card; similar ages, with the man perhaps two or three years older, would argue in favour of rapid capitulation. To ask parents entry to their house would be the surest of all guarantees. Absence likewise *parle au coeur*, if at least it eventually came to an end. A similar provincial origin, especially a village one, would be a sort of reassurance, as if the closely scrutinised orthodoxies and standards of behaviour imposed by the rural collectivity would be likely to be retained even in the city. We will return later to these conventions and, in more detail, to the analysis of those conventions of language, the nuances of emphasis, the delicately shaded promises of happiness (*il m'a fait entrevoir le bonheur*, like a curtain pulled aside to reveal a table groaning with food and foreign wines), or the cruder material arguments, because they tell the historian a great deal more about eighteenth-century *mores*, in an urban or recently urban setting, than they would have told the girls themselves, who, however naïve— and they are naturally primarily concerned to emphasise their naïveté and inexperience—would at least have had a pretty good idea as to what it was all about, just as much as the prudish and *jansénisante Présidente* must eventually have guessed what was the final purpose of Valmont's long-drawn-out and carefully conducted siege. Valmont may not have been an artillery officer, but Laclos was.

Let us then, first of all, discuss our principal source and attempt to assess its reliability, its more obvious traps and falsities, and its eventual value to the social historian concerned to reconstruct the often unstated assumptions of people both very poor, very ignorant, and generally unable to express themselves in reasoned tones. Under an ordinance of Henri III, pregnant girls or women were required to come before a public official at some stage of their pregnancy, generally before the eighth month, in order to make a *déclaration de grossesse*. This obligatory declaration had no doubt not been conceived in the interest of the declarant, though, of course, it might help her to make a paternity claim. What seems much more likely is that the requirement had been imposed in the interest of Authority, in order at least to place some impediment on infanticide, clearly much easier to check in a city than in a rural community, although Olwen Hufton has demonstrated that, given the widespread complicity of certain collectivities, this commonest form of female crime of violence could often be committed with almost complete impunity, and sometimes on a vast scale, in both.[1] The

[1] Olwen Hufton, *The Poor of Eighteenth Century France 1750–1789* (Oxford, 1974).

déclaration de grossesse remained obligatory in the early years of the Revolution, until the introduction of the penal and civil Codes in 1790–1 removed the obligatory character of the statement, converting it into a voluntary one at the choice of the declarant. We find, for instance, one of the declarants, Barbe Condamine, 'fille domestique à Sainte-Julie-en-Beaujolais, demeurant actuellement en cette ville, rue Bourgneuf, chez le Sr. Antoine, cabaretier', in fact the country girl exposed to the dangerous location of a *cabaret*, 'laquelle *pour satisfaire aux ordonnances du royaume* ... a déclaré qu'elle est enceinte d'environ 6 mois et $\frac{1}{2}$ des oeuvres de Jean-Baptiste Perrachon, travailleur de terre, demeurant en ladite paroisse de Julie' (my italics). (Barbe, far from fitting into that much-favoured eighteenth-century literary convention of *les dangers de la ville*, of *la paysanne pervertie*, had lost her virginity before coming to town, had, indeed, no doubt come to town for that very reason; we will return in due course to this important category of country girls who had come to Lyon in order to conceal their shame.) This was on 4 December 1790, right at the beginning of the period of two years covered by our documents. Most such statements would then not have been obligatory, and were made on the initiative of the girls and women, for a variety of reasons, but all primarily for the purpose of identifying the seducer (and it would of course be up to the girl to suggest that there had in fact only been one, while it was commonly argued by each man thus named that, if he had indeed had carnal relations with the declarant, he had been but one of several). After Thermidor and during the Directory a number of judicial authorities, apparently alarmed at the dramatic increase in infanticide both during the revolutionary years, which were also years of considerable libertinage, and during the years of extreme hardship that followed immediately on the Terror, were to put pressure on the Garde des Sceaux in order to induce him to bring in legislation to make the *déclarations* once more obligatory. But the Minister, Merlin de Douai, strongly and successfully resisted such demands, which he rightly described as utterly oppressive, reminiscent of the worse abuses of the old order and smacking of feudal barbarity. At least until the end of the First Republic, such statements were to remain voluntary. Even when they had been obligatory, they would primarily have affected members of the feminine poor : working girls, domestic servants, girls living in lodging houses, their stomachs closely observed for any hint of *rondeurs* by *logeuses* and *concierges* anxious to keep in the good books of the *police des garnies*. For a girl protected in the cocoon of the family unit, as for the girl with affluent parents, it would no doubt have been relatively easy, at least in late eighteenth-century conditions, not only to avoid making an official declaration, but also to dispose of an unwanted pregnancy in some discreet urban establishment. Mercier, with his usual bold jump at figures, and with his usual impudent inaccuracy, was to count 223 such establishments for Paris in the 1780s.

We possess fifty-four such statements, from fifty-two women and girls, two of them, decidedly accident-prone, having turned up twice within periods of eighteen months. All of them are living, at the time, in the area covered by Lyon-Ville (as opposed to Lyon-Campagne, which contained the *faubourgs* and independent *communes* outside the fortifications, as yet intact). Most of the declarants in fact give addresses in the central area, *entre Rhône et Saóne*, either in les Terreaux, in Bellcordière or on the quays. The statements run from 4 December 1790 to 27 November 1792, that is for a period during which the impact of war would scarcely have been felt. It is important to bear this fact in mind, for war and revolution have always been firm allies of masculine designs on women, owing both to the prestige attached to uniforms, especially among female silk-workers, in a garrison town, and to the extra facilities that they would afford to the possibilities of escape on the part of the seducer. On the other hand, thanks to the creation of the National Guard and the expansion of the army, as well as the normal movements of troops—as we shall see, a number of the girls were to claim that they had been seduced by soldiers from the Régiment de la Marck, which had been quartered in the city in 1790—many of the wartime conditions favourable to increased masculine mobility and irresponsibility might be said already to have existed. The figures themselves, month by month, do not appear to have any particular significance, not being sufficiently numerous to bear witness to any sudden increase or decrease : two statements date from December 1790; there are thirty-four for 1791, the most numerous being in March (six) and August (five). There are fifteen *déclarations* for 1792. As, in each case, the duration of the pregnancy is given (*enceinte de six mois, enceinte de huit mois*, and so on), it would no doubt be possible for historians concerned with the degree that religious discipline still prevailed with the poorer elements of the female population to use this kind of source; for, by calculating the dates of conception, the researcher, on the basis of information of this kind, would be in a position, when in possession of a larger body of evidence, stretching over a longer period, to establish to what extent official religious prohibitions of sexual intercourse during the period of Advent were still respected. In this instance, the declarations are not numerous enough to offer any significant clues. But, clearly, this is the sort of problem on which a more extensive use of this type of documentation, over a longer period, and in a number of localities, might offer useful indications as to the relative survival, in one area or another, of the restraints of religious discipline.

Most of the fifty or so girls in the Lyon *dossier* were extremely young, and may indeed have been as innocent and as inexperienced as so many of them were to claim in their statements. Four were seventeen or seventeen and a few months; there were three eighteen-year-olds, three again of nineteen; one gave her age as twenty, one as twenty-one; three were twenty-two. There was one woman of thirty; four were simply described as *filles majeures*, and two as *filles mineures*. Thus most of those—a minority—whose ages were given, were minors. Thirty-one were completely illiterate, being unable to sign their names; twenty-one could at least do this, though the spelling was often erratic (for instance, *Marte* for *Marthe*). As might be expected of women and girls living and working in Lyon, the commonest professional status was employment in some form of silk manufacture: a mass of *ouvrières en soie* and of *brodeuses* and *fileuses*, individual *tireuses*, *dévideuses*, *gazières*, *metteuses en mains*, *apprêteuses*, *ourdisseuses de rubans*, *coupeuses*, *chapelières*, *faiseuses de bourses en soie*: in all, about half the group. Equally predictably, we encounter twelve domestic servants or the sadly eloquent *ex-domestique*. There were two *blanchisseuses*, a *lingère*, an *épicière*, an *ex-cuisinière* (no doubt likewise dismissed as a result of her condition), a *fripière*, a *fille de marchand,* and a *comédienne*, a Lyonnaise who had gone to Marseille to train as an actress and who, according to her account, had succumbed to the attentions of a merchant from that city who had attempted to point out to her dangers inherent in such a profession: to take a leaf out of Fourier's celebrated *Dictionnaire des Cocus* and to attempt a similar enterprise for the many categories of seducer, one might range this gentleman as *le séducteur moralisateur*, a line of approach that seems to have been particularly paying. With the exception of the *fille de marchand*, who seems to have lost the expectation of a considerable sum of money from an aunt, as the result of the shame that she had brought on her family, and the *marchande de modes*, who employed several female apprentices (these came to the court to witness in her favour and to identify her seducer as a man whom they had frequently seen coming up the staircase at dusk, or disappearing down it, 'carrying a packet under his arm' in the early hour at which these girls got up), none of the girls could be said to have had any prospects, other than a marriage that might slightly better their condition (an *ouvrière chapelière*, for instance, seems to have been in hopes of marrying a *marchand chapelier* from her own village, until the young man's parents intervened to point out that he would be marrying beneath him) and a tenuous existence based on very long working hours, followed by a few febrile hours of leisure. For all, a pregnancy would have been an unmitigated disaster. Indeed, one of the themes that emerges most persistently from these sad statements is the humility and the lack of expectancy of most of the declarants; those, for instance, who seem to have faced up to the fact that they were unlikely ever to see their seducers again, because they had gone away, because they were soldiers, pedlars, commercial travellers, hairdressers, medical or veterinary students (the whole range in fact of the more persistent, better-placed eighteenth-century seducer), merely made their statements in order to solicit a place in the foundling hospital for their unborn children (*a demandé un billet pour la Charité*, a phrase that recurs with distressing regularity). There was indeed not much to be expected of a soldier, often only known to the girl under his nickname, nor even of a hairdresser who went under the unhelpful name of *Provençal*.

Departure from home and change of address

A very common accompaniment of a seduction resulting in a pregnancy, the visible sign of having *fauté*, once it had become visible, would be either departure from home, in order to flee the wrath of parents, or, worse still, of brothers, and to escape from the cruel gaze of a tight rural community (*parties de chez elles*—and for such, even the warning of what might befall them in the city, on the favourite ecclesiastical theme among country *curés* of *les dangers de la ville*, might not deter them), or, less dramatic, but equally eloquent, a change of address which, from our documents, can so often be dated from the third or fourth month of pregnancy : sometimes it was only a matter of moving a couple of streets, within the same quarter; more often the girl would take the trouble to move out of the quarter altogether, let us say from one of the narrow streets of les Terreaux to one of the quays. Such changes of address would presumably spell out a dismissal : for instance, a domestic servant, who had been seduced by her employer, or by his son, or by both, would nearly always have been thrown out of the house in which she occupied some wretched attic or cupboard. Her mere presence in her visible condition would have been taken as a form of moral black-mail on the part of her former employers. Barbe Condamine, whom we have already mentioned, as having been seduced by a *pays* from her own village in the Beaujolais, would clearly belong to the former category : she had come to Lyon, when she was six-and-a-half months pregnant, in order perhaps to seek anonymity, and, possibly, to obtain a place for her child. Marianne Motte, 'demeurant ci-devant au Bourg-Argental, de présent à Lyon chez le Sr. Duperrin, son beaufrère, arquebusier, demeurant rue de la Boucherie des Terreaux', who had been seduced by another inhabitant of Bourg-Argental, described as a *bourgeois*, had come to Lyon for a similar purpose, using, like so many provincials of both sexes when first in the city, the family network. There are a great many cases of changes of address within the city, some of them quite explicit : thus 'Françoise André, native de la paroisse de Montluel, fille domestique au service du Sr. Charretier, rue de Trion [her alleged seducer], demeurant actuellement chez la veuve Mathéra, garde-malade, rue de la Barre'. Marie Dangle, *brodeuse*, at the time of her declaration was living with, and working for, her sister, rue de l'Enfant-qui-pisse. Previously 'elle consentit à aller habiter avec le Sr. Flandrin dans un appartement qu'il loua pour elle, place Neuve des Carmes, et elle y a demeuré pendant environ 5 mois'. When she had told Flandrin about her condition, he had thrown her out, and she had then turned to her sister. Marie was luckier than a great many of the *déclarantes* in thus having a close relative in the city. Marie Chirat, the daughter of an inhabitant of la Guillotière, had moved, as a result of her pregnancy, to a room near the porte Saint-Clair, on the road to Geneva, taking the precaution to place the Rhône between herself and her family. Jeanne Rouzon, *lingère*, rue Confort, stated that 'il y a environ un an qu'elle était en apprentissage de sa profession chez la femme du Sr. Canot, tonnelier, demeurant en la paroisse de Caluire'. Canot had seduced her, and she had then moved to the nearby city. Claudine Poncet, 'ouvrière, demeurant chez Mlle Royer, marchande de modes . . . rue Mercière . . . [states that] depuis environ une année et demie elle demeuroit dans la pension où logeoit le Sr. Antoine d'Audiffret', her alleged seducer. Much the same had happened to a girl who had come from the country, with her mother, to Lyon, where they had taken a room in a lodging-house :

Pierrette Blanc . . . demeurant rue Saint-Jean (en avril 1791) [states that] . . . au commencement de l'année dernière elles quittèrent Grézieu-la-Varenne, qu'elles avaient toujours habité, et vinrent se fixer en cette ville, elles prirent un logement dans la maison du Sr. Brigand.

The following year, after having had a child by Brigand, she had moved to la petite rue Tramassac. Anne Burtin, 'ci-devant cuisinière, demeurant chez les demoiselles Reynaud, marchandes de modes, place de la Comédie [se déclare] actuellement logée chez le Sr. Bonneton, ouvrier en soie, place de l'Homme de la Roche'. Benoîte Marduel, who had been a domestic servant of a tradesman, grande rue Mercière, was living in July 1791, rue Tupin. The case of Maria Perrichon, 'dévideuse de soie', is even more explicit :

Demeurant rue Saint-Georges . . . son père compagnon maçon à Neuville . . . [elle] entra au service du Sr. Quet, marchand fabricant . . . place de la Croix-Paquet . . . pendant 4 [mois] et demi qu'elle est restée dans la maison dont elle ne sortit que lorsqu'elle fut convaincue qu'elle était enceinte.

Jeanne Rey, who had gone to Marseille to take up the theatre, and had there met her seducer (*le moralisateur*), who had set her up in a room there, and who had, on learning that she was pregnant, told her that he would be unable to marry her owing to opposition from his family, had returned to Lyon, where she was 'logée en chambre garnie, rue Basse-Ville'. Benoîte Bonnard, living at the time of her statement 'porte Sablet, paroisse Saint-Georges', had had an address in the previous year in the rue Raisin.

Most of these moves can only have been for the worse. For many of these girls, while employed, were likely to have also been housed. Now, in so many of the cases that we have mentioned, they were thrown on to the insecurity, the discomforts and the manifold dangers of a *chambre garnie*, almost certainly shared with several other girls, who, as we shall see from individual examples, would take it in turns to leave the room, on Sundays or feast days, or in the evening, when one of them was receiving her lover. In Lyon, no doubt as an example of the quirks of popular humour, a great many *chambres garnies* were situated at this time either in the rue des Vertus or in the equally inappropriately-styled rue Confort (which is still one of the principal centres of the city's prostitution). And this, then, was likely to be the first of a whole series of changes of addresses, whether as a result of further pregnancies, or of failure to pay the rent. Even the fact of a single change of address may indicate, to the attentive social historian, the principal outward manifestation of a personal tragedy of momentous consequences to the girl concerned. It was a matter of being as it were cast into the outer darkness, removed from the comforting embrace of the family unit, and from the satisfactions of neighbourliness, one of the few compensations of the very poor. It would take little imagination to depict the increasingly desperate journey across the city of a girl thus sent on an ever more rapid quest. Changes of address are certainly more eloquent in *déclarations de grossesse* than in almost any other form of contemporary documentation.

A great many of the country girls who had come to Lyon for one reason or another, once they had discovered their condition, would have been seduced by *pays*, by men from their own localities. In such cases, it would have been quite impossible to conceal what had happened both from the family and from the majority of the locals. For instance, Marianne Faye, 'ouvrière papetière, demeurant ordinairement à Rives (Isère)', where she had worked in a paper mill, had, so she claimed, been seduced by her employer; she adds: 'La comparante a été obligée de quitter sa famille pour venir cacher son malheur et sa honte en cette ville.' Marie Pierry, the daughter of a peasant from Villeurbanne, said that she had been seduced by a gardener, from la Montée de Balmont, paroisse Saint-Didier, in Lyon itself; though he could hardly be described as a *pays,* the girl is likely first to have met him because, like her father, he worked on the land, and was a rustic within the urban community. Even more interesting is the case of Françoise Dubessy, who, on 16 February 1792, says that she was :

> domestique à Lyon, y demeurant, rue Tramassac, âgée de 27 ans ... que depuis son enfance elle était liée avec Jean Biolay, marchand de vin, habitant à Pouilly-le-Monial, ils étaient du même pays, il venait voir la comparante en cette ville, il a profité de l'intimité qui régnait entr'eux depuis si longtems pour ... la séduire ... [elle est] enceinte depuis environ 6 mois de ses oeuvres.

We learn from another source that the wine-merchant had been in the habit of walking the very considerable distance from Pouilly-le-Monial to Lyon to see Françoise every other Sunday. The girl, who clearly had had her eye on such an advantageous match for a very long time—they had known each other for over ten years—took this assiduity as a guarantee of the seriousness of the man's intentions. What is more, her workmates had met him on a number of these occasions.

Jeanne Rouzon, whom we have already mentioned, stated, in May 1791, that while working in Caluire, her birthplace,

> elle y a fit la connoissance du nommé François Bergeron, garçon cordonnier, demeurant actuellement en ce bourg, chez le Sr. Laurent, marchand cordonnier ... que cependant voilà près de 8 jours qu'il a cessé de la voir, sans aucun sujet de mécontentement si ce n'est que sa position ne lui permettant de rester plus longtems sans terminer la promesse qu'il lui a si souvent réiterée, elle le pressoit vivement à ses fins, ce qui peut peut-être l'en avoir éloigné.

The poor girl, though illiterate, was clearly no fool.

There are two further instances of alleged seduction by *pays* from two localities much nearer Lyon, indeed on the very outskirts of the city. The first concerns 'Dlle. Isabelle Collonge, fille mineure, apprentie gazière, demeurant en ce canton [Cuire] chez le Sr. Germain Poisson, laquelle a dit que ce dernier, chez lequel elle est apprentie, l'a séduite'. The other is that of a girl from the *commune* of la Guillotière, a place which, owing to the number of its *guinguettes* and its popularity with the inhabitants of the central peninsula as a week-end resort and as a centre for Saturday and Sunday *bals,* must have accounted for a very large number of pregnancies :

> Marguerite Terrier, tailleuse, demeurant au faubourg de la Guillotière, chez Sr. François Terrier, son père, chirurgien juré [déclare] ... qu'elle a eu le malheur de se lier avec Pierre Landouard, élève de l'école royale vétérinaire

établie aud. faubourg...à peine la remontrante était-elle enceinte qu'il est
parti de ce pays promettant, il est vrai, de bientôt revenir, mais bien résolu
cependant de fuir à jamais celle qu'il avait séduite.

This is perhaps not quite the case of a girl succumbing to the usual
arguments of a compatriot, arguments which would normally go much
as follows: 'A Pâques (ou à Noël) on retournera au pays pour s'y marier
et pour s'y fixer.' For her seducer was only a *casual* inhabitant of la
Guillotière, and was thus better protected than most more stationary
male seducers. But it is fairly clear that the two must have met both as
a result of the presence of the school in the *faubourg* and because her
father would no doubt have had many acquaintances in medical circles.

Both the victims themselves and what might be described as accepted
popular opinion, and the sort of parallel popular justice that would
operate as a form of community pressure in such matters and that was
often more effective than the official system of rewards and penalties,
were particularly severe on men who were seen to have profited from
the fact that they had been from the same village in order to capture
the confidence of the object of their lust. They had, in some way, sinned
against the collectivity, as well as against the girl. Indeed, their force of
persuasion would if anything have increased in the alien setting of a
large city, in which people from the same village would naturally tend
to be thrown together—and there was every likelihood in a city as
geographically localised by quarter, trade and provincial origin as Lyon
that they would in fact often be living in close proximity, in the same
street or even in the same lodging-house—and in which links *entre
gens du pays* would become all the more insistent as a form of self-
defence and mutual help. Seductions of this type seem to have been
regarded as a particularly obnoxious form of *escroquerie morale*, in
that the girl's defences would be down almost before the operation had
been undertaken.

Masculine mobility and flight

For the man, on the other hand, especially if unattached, there would
always be an easy way out of a situation in which he was being asked
to accept responsibility for paternity: he merely had to leave the city,
generally after a long string of promises, including that of a forwarding
address which, in most cases, would never be forwarded. Any exceptional
external factors, such as war or revolution, that would increase masculine
mobility would be likely both to render the potential seducer more
enterprising, more indifferent to the inevitable fate of the girl, and to
offer him a number of socially acceptable channels of escape, the most

acceptable, at *any* period, being enlistment. And there was not much that a girl could do about a seducer who was already in the army, or who was a medical or veterinary student, or, equally, who travelled for his living. The Lyon *déclarations de grossesse* offer a sad, repetitive, but indeed predictable chronicle of departure, *absent de la ville,* and so on, in this respect, very much on the old, old theme of *parti sans laisser d'adresse,* save that, in most instances, they had indeed promised the girl to send one on, once they had found a settled abode.

Le Sr. Tournachon (marchand libraire, Grande Rue Mercière) prétexta qu'il avait un voyage et qu'il ne pouvait être en cette ville que vers la fin de mai dernier [and we are now in mid-July] ... Depuis, la comparante est instruite que le Sr. Tournachon est en cette ville, quoiqu'il fasse dire qu'il est encore absent.

Tournachon was of course *bound* to come back, attached as he was to les Terreaux by the possession of a prosperous business in books and stationery. He had, in this instance, only gained a temporary respite; and he must have been singularly thoughtless, or equally careless, to have believed that his return would pass unnoticed by his former servant, Benoîte Marduel, whom he had allegedly seduced, and who, at the time of his unheralded return, was living a few doors away from the rue Mercière, in the rue Tupin. In this closed community of les Terreaux, the steep, narrow streets turning in on one another in a confused jumble of *montées* and *descentes,* steps, *traboules,* slopes so steep as to necessitate the provision of chains for the pedestrian to hold on to, nothing would pass unnoticed, especially the return of an important tradesman. Tournachon in fact decided in the end to sit it out and to deny everything. It was his word against that of his former servant. And would not the mere fact that he had dismissed her (had *had* to dismiss her, he would add) have witnessed against her, with its suggestion of moral turpitude or professional incompetence? Le Sr. Tournachon, a man of his standing in his quarter, would not have much to fear from a discharged servant, save perhaps the occasional embarrassing encounter, rue Tupin, and strident insults coming from a seventh storey, or from the black entry to a *traboule,* rue Mercière or rue Bouteille, delivered by the Dlle. Marduel herself or by one of her numerous workmates. But this is in fact an exceptional case, in that the man *did* come back. In most instances, the men did not, though they had left saying that they would—*incessamment, en peu de tems quand il sera établi, quand il aura terminé ses affaires, quand il aura visité sa famille, quand il aura l'accord de ses parents, quand il aura mis de côté une somme suffisante,* the formal rigmarole of *escroquerie sur l'avenir,* a sort of masculine *fuite en avant,* merely to gain time—a few weeks or a few months—a pathetic example of masculine cowardice, or of a sense of guilt in which the main concern is to hide a few blushes.

Here is Virginie Bergeon, naturally *ci-devant domestique*, because she belongs as by right to that class of almost professional candour :

> demeurant à présent à l'hôtel de Provence... 22 ans... [déclare] qu'elle est enceinte d'environ 5 mois des oeuvres du nommé *Joseph*, soldat qui a été en semestre en cette Ville pendant 5 mois, et qui s'est absenté de cette Ville depuis Pâques [and it is now 18 May], led. Joseph devant revenir dans quelques tems en cette Ville, la comparante ne doit rien négliger pour assurer l'état de son enfant.

The poor girl does not even know the fellow's full name. She is not likely ever to see him again; and she would do as well to ask for a ticket for *la Charité*.

Louise Verchère, *blanchisseuse de bas,* aged 25, domiciled place du Change, is less optimistic, or, perhaps, more realistic, for she at least knows that *her* seducer is unlikely ever to show his face again in Lyon : '[déclare] qu'elle est enceinte de 8 mois et $\frac{1}{2}$ des oeuvres d'un garcon perruquier nommé *Provençal,* actuellement absent de cette ville, et qu'elle est dans l'intention de se procurer un billet de l'hôpital de la Charité pour y placer l'enfant', clearly the only possible solution when the alleged seducer was known to the girl only under the name of *Provençal.*

Then there is the case of Annette Dementhon, 'fille du Sr. Dementhon, marchand de dorures fausses, demeurant à Lyon, âgée de 17 ans', a girl who had been unlucky enough to have taken up with a commercial traveller :

> ...qu'il y a environ un an elle fit la connoissance du Sr. Jaivry, voyageur pour le commerce de cette ville à Bordeaux, et habitant alternativement dans l'une ou l'autre de ces deux villes... il lui fit des propositions de mariage, il n'attendait, disait-il, que le moment où il auroit pu parvenir à arranger des affaires de manière à pouvoir se fixer absolument à Lyon. Le Sr. Jaivry se ménageant de tems à autres des entrevues avec la comparante à l'insu de ses parens... il lui a annoncé qu'il retournoit à Bordeaux pour arranger ses affaires et revenir immédiatement demander sa main à ses parens.
>
> Le Sr. Jaivry, en partant, annonça à la comparante qu'elle recevrait incessamment de ses nouvelles, et qu'il lui donneroit des addresses sûres pour qu'elle pût lui écrire; cependant deux mois se sont écoulés et elle est encore dans l'attente, le Sr. Jaivry a gardé le plus profond silence. La comparante a lieu d'être étonnée, mais il lui importe d'assurer l'existence de l'enfant.

Of all the men mentioned in this repetitious chronicle of departures, Jaivry was perhaps the best placed professionally thus to opt out, without any material damage to himself.

There are one or two examples of the man persuading the girl to leave, promising to follow on at a later date. This is what happened to the would-be actress, after she had met her *séducteur moralisateur* :

Jeanne Rey, de présent à Lyon, logée en chambre garnie, rue Basse Ville . . . qu'au mois d'août 1789, elle partit de cette ville pour se rendre à Marseille dans l'intention d'y jouer la comédie, arrivée dans cette dernière ville, elle se disposoit à exécuter le projet qu'elle avait formé lorsqu'un Sr. Pierre François Plurnel Laguille, négotiant en ladite ville . . . fit connoissance de la comparante dans une maison à laquelle elle étoit recommandée . . . à force de sollicitations il parvint à la dégoûter de son état et à la recevoir habituellement dans un appartement qu'il lui a loué à Marseille aux fêtes de Pâques 1789 [1790?] . . . il lui a témoigné que des raisons de famille et des interêts de commerce exigeaient qu'elle vînt faire ses couches en cette ville [de Lyon].

Plurnel Laguille, no doubt a man of substance, once he had learnt of his mistress's condition, was almost indecently anxious to see her out of the way, and on the road north. There was absolutely no likelihood that he would ever be following her there.

And so it goes on: 'Marie Faton, blanchisseuse . . . demeurant rue des Forges . . . 19 ans . . . enceinte d'environ 7 mois des oeuvres du Sr. François Revelain, crocheteur, absent de cette ville'; 'François Perchon, apprentie tailleuse . . . demeurant chez la femme Genon, rue Longue . . . 20 ans . . . enceinte d'environ 4 mois et $\frac{1}{2}$ des oeuvres du Sr. Pinjon, perruquier, actuellement absent de cette ville' (she does not insist but asks for a *billet pour l'hôpital*); 'Louise Nardy, tireuse de soie à Lyon, y demeurant, rue Mercière . . . enceinte depuis près de 6 mois des faits & oeuvres du Sr. Grégoire, Sergent au Régiment de la Marck', who, by February 1791, had left Lyon; 'Pernon Prévôt, brodeuse . . . demeurant rue Sainte-Catherine . . . âgée de 18 ans . . . qu'il y a environ 8 mois qu'elle fit la connoissance d'un Sr. Enstremanny, marchand suisse, pour lors en cette ville . . . il est absent de cette ville, elle espère qu'il ne l'abandonnera pas.' But it is unlikely that the *marchand helvète* will be seen in Lyon again, or at least rue Sainte-Catherine, right in the middle of les Terreaux, where everything is at once known and in which his presence would at once be spotted by dozens of Pernon's workmates in silk. 'Anne Burtin, ci-devant cuisinière . . . demeurant chez les Dlles Reynaud, marchandes de modes, place de la Comédie, actuellement logée chez le Sr. Bonneton, ouvrier en soie, place de l'Homme de la roche . . . enceinte depuis environ 5 mois et $\frac{1}{2}$ des oeuvres de Jean Lespinasse, garçon perruquier, engagé dans les volontaires nationaux et absent de cette ville' (*billet pour l'hôpital*).

The alleged seducer of Françoise Dueure, *brodeuse*, Bavet, 'marchand drapier, associé du Sr. Gaillard . . . rue de Saint-Nizier', a man whom we have already encountered in his category as *séducteur correspondant,* has this to say :

> ...il lui dit qu'il partoit pour voyage et qu'à son retour qui devoit être prochain, il lui donneroit sa main... de retour en cette ville depuis 8 jours, lorsqu'elle l'a pressé de nouveau de tenir la parole... il a pris le parti de faire sur le champ un nouveau voyage.

Françoise, who was a *brodeuse,* must have had illusions of grandeur if she had really believed that a *marchand drapier* would marry her in order to regularise her situation. But Bavet must also have been extremely imprudent if he believed that his return would pass unnoticed : for he lived in the rue Saint-Nizier, while Françoise had an address, quai de Saône, just round the corner.

Jeanne Caillot, *brodeuse,* living rue Plat-d'Argent, and the oldest of the women in this group—she was thirty—had been ready to believe that her age would in fact argue in her favour with the man who had shown a persistent interest in her over a period of years, and who seems to have played a waiting game, till finally cornered :

> ...qu'il y a nombre d'années que le commerce de broderies a amené dans son domicile le Sr. Claude-Marie Desvernai, commis chez le Sr. Sonnet, marchand brodeur...led. Desvernai a depuis longtems proposé à la comparante de l'épouser, comme l'état et l'âge de ce dernier, qui est âgé de quarante ans, étaient très sortables, la comparante a cru aux promesses dud. Desvernai...le Sr. Desvernai, loin de tenir sa parole, s'est absenté.

though, as a *commis brodeur,* he cannot have gone very far. Perhaps he merely moved up the hill to la Croix-Rousse, where he might have expected to obtain employment in his trade.

Benoîte Bonnard, *coupeuse de poils pour la chapellerie,* appears to have driven her alleged seducer away, back to his village, by being too pressing, and by setting her work mates on to him to remind him of his duties :

> La grossesse s'avançant la remontrante a été plus pressante pour l'engager à tenir ses promesses, mais Pierre Dusurgey a abandonné la ville et est allé s'établir maître chapelier à Mornant. Alors la reclamante lui a fait écrire [for she was illiterate] et a fait faire auprès de lui différentes démarches. Pierre Dusurgey a été sourd à ses sollicitations.

However, this was not quite the end of this liaison. For we learn from one of the witnesses, Brossard, *cordonnier,* who had gone for walks with the couple, que Pierre Dusurgey étoit très lié avec la plaignante, au point que lorsque led. Dusurgey s'est retiré à Mornant, sa patrie, il venoit tous les 15 jours voir la plaignante, que sur la fin de novembre dernier [and it is now mid-February] sachant que la plaignante étoit enceinte, lue témoin en parla aud. Dusurgey, que ce dernier sembloit douter que ce fût de ses oeuvres, disant cependant qu'il épouseroit volontiers le plaignante si ses parents de lui Dusurgey ne s'y opposoit pas.

It was perhaps an easy and rather cowardly way out, for it is evident that the parents of a *maître chapelier* would be unlikely to favour their son's marriage to a girl working as a mere *coupeuse de poils.* It was on occasions such as these that the pull of the native village might become irresistible. Dusurgey was fortunate in thus possessing a line of retreat to the nearby village of Mornant, within walking distance of Lyon, though there was the possible danger that Benoîte might be tempted to do the journey in the opposite direction and go and seek him out there, and confront his parents and relatives with the spectacle of her condition.

La Dlle. Chirat, metteuse en mains ... demeurant près de la porte Saint-Clair ... [se porte] en déclaration de grossesse contre le Sr. Bouillier, natif de la ville de Lons-le-Saunier ... commis facteur chez le Sr. Talon fils & Mollière négotiants de cette ville ... Le Sr. Bouillier [she adds enviously] est déjà riche par le décès de son père et de son oncle ... [She herself] fille mineure de défunt Sr. Chirat, bourgeois à la Guillotière ... enceinte depuis environ 8 mois ... état qui l'a brouillée (avec assez de raison) avec sa famille, et principalement avec une tante de laquelle elle a beaucoup à espérer.

She has an apprentice of eighteen who witnesses to Bouillier's assiduities, adding that he had not come to see her since January; and it was now March. He had in fact gone back to Lons. La Dlle. Chirat, who was in the trade, should perhaps have known better than to have taken up with the travelling representative of an important firm based on Lons, because it should have been clear to her that his regular employment offered him an easy line of retreat back to the Jura. The nature of his work would indeed have made it very likely that he only came to Lyon for limited periods, to contact manufacturers for his employers. Marie Chirat may also have felt that her prospects would be improved by the fact that, like her alleged seducer, she was fatherless and that, having a female apprentice, she was far from representing a losing proposition.

Gasparde Latour, *brodeuse,* certainly has no cause for hope; for, a year previously, she had taken up with a *perruquier,* and as so often happens to those in that highly mobile trade, he had gone long since on his way.

Dlle. Claudine Poncet, ouvrière demeurant chez Mlle Royer, marchande de modes... rue Mercière [déclare] que depuis environ une année et ½ la déclarante demeuroit dans la pension où logeoit le Sr. Antoine d'Audiffret... depuis quelques tems il a quitté la ville, cependant la remontrante, âgée à peine de 17 ans, n'a perdu son honneur que faute d'expérience.

There is not much hope for her either. The case of Louise Perenne is likewise sadly straightforward, witnessing as it does both for the likeliest inception of a liaison and the most probable outcome of its course, once she was pregnant. She was a domestic servant who worked for the *maître des postes aux chevaux* of Villefranche-sur-Saône, on the high-road from Lyon to Paris. Her father was a *vigneron* in the same town. Nine or ten months before her statement, she had become acquainted, in the course of her work, with 'Sr. Joseph Castaing, maître tailleur du régiment appellé ci-devant Guyenne, en garnison à Villefranche'. The poor girl was likely to be fair game for any passing soldier, for to be the servant of a *maître des postes* would be almost as perilous as to be a *fille de salle* in an inn on one of the great military highroads. Nor would she ever be likely to catch up with Castaing, and with the *régiment ci-devant Guyenne,* which by this time, in late December 1791, would have long since left Villefranche, a town which, in any case, never had a permanent garrison, being, unlike Lyon, merely a *lieu d'étape.*

The statement made by Dlle. Marie Maillot, *fille épicière,* 'demeurant rue du Puits de Sel', is likewise of more general interest, as it illustrates not only the by now only too familiar theme of masculine *dérobage,* villainy, cowardice, or selfishness, in the usual forms of departure or going to earth; it also suggests a compensatory solidarity among the poor and the humble; for Marie, in her efforts to bring her lover to accept his responsibilities, enlists the support of a female witness, no doubt a workmate, certainly a neighbour, as she appears to be very much aware of the previous comings and goings of the couple, and who agrees to go and see the man, on Marie's behalf, in an effort to appeal to what sense of duty he may have possessed. Marie herself says

que depuis environ 8 mois, un Sr. Benoît Bergoz, compagnon charpentier chez le Sr. Boeuf, place Saint-Jean... est parvenu à la séduire et a habité son domicile avec assiduité, mais lorsque la remontrante est devenue enceinte... celui-ci a cessé ses fréquentes visites, et depuis peu il l'a entièrement abandonnée.

It is at this point that the witness takes up the account:

... que la veille de Noël [we are now in February 1792] dernière la dlle. Maillot vint chez la déposante où elle resta pendant trois semaines, c'est-à-dire jusqu'au milieu de janvier dernier, que pendant ce tems elle a vu venir trois

fois le Sr. Bergoz qui s'entretenait avec lad. Maillot, que cette dernière dit à la
déposante qu'elle devait se marier à Pâques avec led. Bergoz, qu'elle déposante
est depuis allée chez led. Bergoz de la part de la dlle. Maillot pour l'engager
à venir parler à cette dernière, qu'il lui répondit qu'il alloit s'y rendre et que
lad. Maillot n'avoit qu'à l'attendre chez la déposante, mais led. Bergoz ne s'y
rendit point.

It would have been rather astonishing, having himself fixed the meeting
place, and knowing that he would have to face both girls, if he *had*
indeed turned up.

The remaining chronicle of woe, injured innocence and hopelessness
is entirely predictable. Pierrette Carret, 'tailleuse, enceinte depuis environ
7 mois des oeuvres du Sr. Gochon, officier dans les volontaires, actuellement absent', asks for *un billet pour la Charité*. Marie Béatrix,
'demeurant rue des Trois Ecuries', names as her seducer Philippe
Gandin, 'ci-devant domicilié à Lyon, demeurant actuellement à Mon-
tagny'. Another obliging female workmate comes to the aid of Dlle.
Marie Persan 'fille majeure, dévideuse . . . demeurant rue Saint-Cosme',
who had succumbed to the arguments of Laurent Giret, 'ouvrier en soie,
demeurant rue Ferrandière'; she states

qu'il y a environ deux mois, se trouvant chez la fille Persan sur environ 7
heures du soir, elle vit entrer Laurent Giret, que la fille Persan fit sortir une
ouvrière [for, at this level of society, to be alone with someone is something
of a luxury that needs to be planned and that is dependent on the goodwill
of other workmates] et quand elle se trouva seule avec la déposante et Laurent
Giret, elle dit en pleurant à ce dernier qu'il étoit bien tems de prendre des
arrangemens relativement à l'enfant dont elle était enceinte par ses faits, que
Laurent Giret répondit qu'elle étoit folle, qu'elle n'était sûrement pas enceinte
que led. Giret paraissant vouloir s'en aller, la fille Persan chercha à la retenir,
mais il la poussa avec brutalité sur des fagots, que la déposante lui observa
qu'un honnête homme ne se conduisit pas ainsi avec une fille dont il avait
joui, à quoi led. Giret ne répondit rien et se retira.

—a case, by no means rare in this brutal world of masculine violence,
of employing force as well as escape tactics. Claudine Gariot, *dévideuse
de soie,* states that she is pregnant 'des oeuvres du nommé Vivien, garçon
chapelier, duquel elle ignore la demeure'. Having no illusions, she asks
for her ticket. Catherine Sapin, another *dévideuse,* 'demeurant rue Henri,
chez le Sr. Solary, maître fabricant en étoffes de soie, [se déclare] enceinte
des oeuvres de Jean Robin, cordonnier, absent'. Jeanne Rey, *brodeuse,*
accuses a former *commis aux octrois,* 'actuellement absent de cette ville';
Marie Pierrette Blanc,

habitante de la Guillotière, dépendante de l'autorité de son père, enceinte
des oeuvres de François Antoine Haley fils cadet, demeurant rue de la

Monnaie, ce jeune homme avoit promis de l'épouser, il a reçu de Pierre Blanc [the girl's father] une somme considérable pour fournir à la dot... ce jeune home paraît vouloir tromper lad. Marie Pierrette Blanc, car il s'est absenté.

He had indeed a double reason for disappearing from the scene, once he had laid hands on the money.

Perhaps the last word on the subject of masculine mobility should come from a document of a different nature, and from a different city, in the form of a *certificat d'indigence* delivered by the *comité de bienfaisance* of the Section des Arcis, in Paris, on 22 Thermidor Year III (9 August 1795), in favour of a former nun who had married:

> ...[déclare] avoir délivré le présent certificat d'indigence à la citoyenne *Anne-Louise Droz*, ex-religieuse, âgée de 32 ans environ, et depuis 18 mois femme du citoyen Charles Mollet, *perruquier chambrelant* [perhaps only an ex-nun in her innocence and inexperience of the ways of the world could have joined forces with an itinerant hairdresser, whose trade took him from house to house, allowing him, any moment, a convincing excuse for absence!] demeurant rue de la Poterie No. 6... mais dont le chagrin causé tant par le défaut de pratiques que par la circonstance des temps difficiles, a fortement [?] porté led. C. Mollet à délaisser sa femme enceinte de six mois avec un enfant d'un an environ, pour s'en aller courir le pays, après avoir vendu jusqu'aux cendres du feu, ce qui composait leur petit ménage, et de plus avoir contraint son épouse à consentir à l'engagement du brevet de pension de 500 livres qui lui avait été délivrée par l'Etat, pour l'indemniser des avant ages qu'elle [sic] jouissait en conventualité... ladite citoyenne... véritablement malheureuse, tant par son inexpérience et bonhomie que par le délaissement de son époux... n'ayant même de quoi coucher ni son enfant, elle est réléguée dans un cabinet garni, rue de la Verrerie, 100.[1]

Such was the lot of an ex-nun, living in a sort of cupboard—in one of the worst lodging-houses of the rue de la Verrerie, a street which, with its prolongation of the rue des Lombards, was notorious for these flea-pits and for the rapid turn-over of population that they contained— abandoned by her husband 'pour s'en aller courir le pays, après avoir vendu jusqu'aux cendres du feu', while she had to look after a child of one and face up to an immediate future in which there would soon be a second one, and that to be born in the bitter month of November 1795: and even she could not have foreseen, from the depth of her misery and pessimism, just how bitter that winter was going to be. Perhaps the most surprising thing about this statement on the subject of the double standard is the ex-nun's resignation. There is scarcely a

---

[1] *A.N.* F 15 2820 (comité de bienfaisance de la Section des Arcis, attestation datée du 22 thermidor an III).

hint of criticism of her husband's conduct towards her, and she seems to take his departure, to enjoy the freedom and adventure of the open road, almost as a matter of course. Or perhaps it is not so surprising after all. Aged thirty-two, and presumably released from her vows in her late twenties, she had had a long schooling in self-abnegation. And, in the famine year of 1795, and in the absence of *les pratiques,* what else remained for a *perruquier chambrelant* to do, other than to enlist or to take to the roads, the usual alternatives that Swift reserves for his discharged footman butler?[1] For Droz, rather than walking from house to house, with his brush, his razor, his bowl and his towel, it would now be a matter of trying his luck on the highroads, perhaps on the fringes of Army service—*transports militaires, habillement,* or even in his own profession, in the wake of the *armée du Nord.* One way or another, and with the prospect opening out before him of endless encounters with *filles de salle,* as he headed towards the old borders, he would no doubt soon have forgotten his wife and child and future offspring, and the damp and wretched rue de la Verrerie. War, famine and cold formed a trinity that, in eighteenth-century conditions, offered the most persuasive incentive to masculine selfishness and opting out.

I have not yet quite finished with this theme of escape: *absent de cette ville, parti sans laisser d'adresse, actuellement dans les volontaires nationaux.* For of course, it was not *always* the man who was at fault—the girls who made their statements had to name a man, *one* man, but he would not necessarily be the right one. And they would, if in the slightest bit calculating, be more likely to name a man of some substance than a workmate who could hardly be expected to do anything very much for them in their present condition. There was a masculine point of view, too; and it was not necessarily a false or selfish one. 'Why pick on me,' the man might ask, 'when it is well known that la Dlle. in question accorded her favours to a whole quarter?' And flight was not always accomplished alone. The most agreeable form of travel would not be flight at all, but *à deux,* at a stage of the relationship before pregnancy had reduced the girl's mobility and had given the man a powerful motive to get right away. It is these two subjects that we should now consider, before moving on to the strategy and language of seduction as employed by the male.

---

[1] 'To grow old in the office of a footman, is the highest of all indignities ... I directly advise you to go upon the road, which is the only post of honour left you : there you will meet many of your old comrades, and live a short life and a merry one, and make a figure at your exit, wherein I will give you some instructions.
The last advice I give you, relates to your behaviour when you are going to be hanged; which ... may very probably be your lot.'

Even the judicial authorities, who had so often been in a position to transcribe the sad monologues of these ill-used women, were not always entirely sympathetic to the *déclarantes*. When for instance, Marie Dangle, *brodeuse*, aged $17\frac{1}{2}$ and nine months pregnant, accuses the Sr. Flandrin, whom, characteristically, she had met at her sister's, a girl older than herself, the judge points out to her: 'A elle représenté qu'il paraît qu'elle a été séduite bien facilement, puisqu'il n'y a eu que peu d'intervalle entre la connaissance qu'elle a faite du Sr. Flandrin et l'époque de sa grossesse'. She had met Flandrin at her sister's ten months previously, so that what she calls her *première imprudence* must have occurred very soon after this meeting; and she admits that, soon afterwards, she allowed Flandrin, who seems to have been a man of some substance, to set her up in a room of her own, the rent of which he paid, and where he came regularly to see her. Her reply to the judge's remarks was: 'Répond que la promesse que le Sr. Flandrin lui avait faite de l'épouser, et surtout l'amitié qu'il était parvenue à lui inspirer ont causé sa faiblesse.' Flandrin had certainly been a fast operator. But the judge was perhaps being rather hard on a girl not yet eighteen.

The commonest masculine point of view is best expressed by Clémence Bonnenfant, 'boulanger à Lyon, y demeurant, rue Groslée . . . 24 ans':

> . . . qu'il ne disconvient pas d'avoir eu des familiarités, avec Pierrette Chapuis (domestique), mais nous assure qu'il ne lui a jamais promis de l'épouser, qu'il y a entr'eux une trop grande différence d'âge pour penser à un établissement aussi malassorti puisque lad. Chapuis a au moins 10 ans de plus que lui [she is one of the few girls who does not give her age in her statement] . . . qu'il serait injuste de le déclarer père de l'enfant de cette fille, puisqu'elle lui est convenue avoir eu des liaisons avec d'autres que lui.

Bonnenfant was being ungallant, but if la Chapuis was indeed thirty-four, she may indeed have had designs on the young man.

We have an obvious case in which a former servant attempted to saddle her one-time employer with the paternity of a child who seems to have been fathered in fact by the man with whom she was living at the time of her statement:

> Jean-Marie Morel, demeurant à Lyon, place des Cordeliers, paroisse Saint-Nizier . . . [dépose] qu'il vient d'apprendre qu'une fille qui demeuroit chez lui il y a environ 5 ans en qualité de domestique nommée *Josèphe* dont il ignore le nom de famille, a rendu contre lui une plainte en paternité de l'enfant dont elle se dit enceinte.
>
> Cette accusation n'est qu'une pure calomnie machinée entre cette fille et le nommé Duret, matelassier, avec lequel elle habite, et d'autres personnes, leurs fauteurs et adhérens. En effet, le suppliant vient d'apprendre que cette fille loge dans une chambre, rue Neuve, qu'elle se fait nommer femme Duret, et qu'en effet led. Duret vit logé et couché avec elle.

And another witness is even more precise :

François Martin, colporteur ... 50 ... ans ... rue Neuve ... dépose qu'il ne sait autre chose ... si ce n'est que la fille *Josèphe* habite une chambre dans la maison Poirat, rue Neuve, depuis environ 2 mois, que lui témoin habitant dans la même maison et porte à porte sur le même palier, il a vu presque tous les jours le nommé Duret, matelassier, venir chez lad. fille *Josèphe*, ne sait le témoin si led. Duret couchait dans l'appartement où il venoit ordinairement sur les 10 heures du soir ... ajoute ... que la fille *Josèphe* se faisoit appeller femme Duret, que depuis 8 jours la fille *Josèphe* n'a pas couché dans son appartement.

Martin is followed by his wife and two daughters; all prove very unsympathetic witnesses to the girl Josèphe, showing her up as a pretentious liar and an impostor, whom they appear to have regarded as a disgrace to the neighbourhood. There is certainly very little they seem to have missed about the girl's habits and statements, and there is a certain glee in their eagerness to unmask her. *La femme* Martin, *brodeuse,* also aged 50, states

qu'il y a environ 2 mois que la fille désignée ... de *Josèphe* est venue habiter une chambre ... que le nommé Duret ... s'est aidé au transport des meubles de cette fille, elle déposante l'ayant rencontré dans l'escalier portant un matelas, qu'il est à la connoissance de la déposante que led. Duret mangeait souvent avec la fille *Josèphe*, lui apportait du pain et y couchait fréquemment, que la déposante ayant quelques fois exprimé sa surprise à la fille *Josèphe* sur ce que le Sr. Duret, son mari, couchait quelques fois hors de chez elle [this is rather more than neighbourly concern], la fille *Josèphe* lui observait que son mari, en raison de son état de matelassier, étoit souvent obligé de coucher chez les maîtres qui l'occupaient, et la déposante a appris depuis environ 3 semaines que led. Duret n'est point le mari de la fille *Josèphe*, ayant ouï dire que led. Duret a femmt et enfant, et qu'il demeure rue Téraille, ajoute la déposante avoir vu une femme boîteuse et d'un âge avancé qu'on lui a dit être la véritable femme Duret et une jeune fille âgée de 10 à 11 ans ... en le désignant sous la qualification de son père.

The two daughters of the Martin family back up their mother's testimony with evident satisfaction and plenty of malice. Françoise, also a *brodeuse,* aged 23, states

que lad. fille ... s'y est annoncée comme femme mariée, et sous le nom de femme Duret, que sur l'observation faite par la déposante à lad. femme Duret qu'elle n'avoit point de bague de mariage, cette dernière lui répondit qu'elle était mariée depuis un an, mais qu'elle avait été obligée de vendre sa bague par nécessité.

The elder daughter, Claudine, 24, likewise *brodeuse,* backs up her

sister's statement, adding the interesting piece of information 'qu'elle a
même ouï dire que led. Duret avait une loquetière de la porte d'allée',
that is, that he could open the wooden door of the *traboule* leading to
the staircase that gave access to the storey, so that he would have been
able to let himself in at any time, day or night.

Finally, yet another inhabitant of the house, Marie Piard, a 24-year-
old *dévideuse de soie*—there is a solidarity among the four silk workers
who are witnesses, and that seems best to express itself in scarcely concealed hostility to the so-called *femme* Duret, who, it seems clear, was
not in the trade—makes her contribution to the demolition of Josèphe:

> que la fille *Josèphe* habite une chambre au 5me étage . . . ayant vu led. Duret
> entrer le soir et sortir le matin, ajoute la déposante que s'étant liée en raison
> du voisinage avec la fille *Josèphe*, cette dernière lui a fait ses confidences, et
> lui a dit qu'elle n'était pas mariée avec led. Duret, qu'étant enceinte depuis
> plusieurs mois, elle devait faire sa déclaration sur un inconnu, mais que quel-
> ques tems aprés la fille *Josèphe* lui fit part du projet qu'elle avait de désigner
> dans sa plainte le Sr. Morel.

One cannot help feeling rather sorry for Josèphe, so completely
caught up in her web of lies and contradictions, her pathetic inventions
(why, one might ask, would a *matelassier*, of all people, be expected
to work at night, *chez les maîtres,* who would presumably be using their
own mattresses to get a bit of sleep? He might, of course, have been
expected to deliver mattresses, according to need, at nightfall, but this
would hardly account for his absence throughout the night), her uncon-
vincing suggestion that she had pawned her ring, an old, old fable on
the part of girls in her situation; and harried with such sustained questioning and close observation by the three women in the Martin family
—the father seems to have been rather more indulgent and rather less
observant, but then he would have had less inclination to stand around,
sur le palier, and gossip with the imprudent girl—and by the other
brodeuse. One suspects that the women at least had spotted from the
start that there was something irregular in the girl's situation, and had
then decided to play her along, in an effort to find out more, and to
trap her in her contradictory statements. *La femme* Martin, in particular, must have gone to considerable trouble to identify the deformed
woman and her ten-year-old daughter, asking her workmates, or making
enquiries in this or other quarters, as she delivered half-finished goods,
or went out to take orders from *marchands de soie.* It is possible, too,
that the Martins worked as a family unit. *La femme* Duret, the real one,
who was said to be antique, and who walked with a limp, would have
been a figure widely identified in this heavily populated, close-packed,
and closely observed area, each of the long black windows hacked out of

the tall ochre-coloured seven- or eight-storey buildings acting as so many observatories for what went on in the dark gulleys of the street, far below, as well as offering an excellent *vue plongeante* into shadowy interiors, at the level of the storey, or a little below it. Lyon was not a shuttered town, and only in the hot months would the interiors be partly hidden from indiscreet gaze by brightly striped awnings. Perhaps the principal interest to us of the doings of *la fille Josèphe*, as observed by the Martins, is not whether she was out to ensnare her former employer, the no doubt substantial Morel. That would be her concern, not ours. But the episode abundantly illustrates several themes to which we will return later : the community of the staircase and the promiscuity of *le palier*—how often, in these statements, do we hear witnesses who live opposite a room, on the same landing, and who, getting up very early, or returning from work in the evening, are able to observe all the comings and goings of their neighbours, even to such details as a table laid for two places *pour le souper;* the solidarity within a given trade, a solidarity that would often be transformed into suspicion or hostility when facing outwards; the fact that women are generally more severe than men in their judgments on sexual irregularity, especially when the sinner is herself a woman; the pattern, through the day, of occasional conversation, during a pause *sur le palier;* the ability to read much into apparently simple acts—that, for instance, of carrying a mattress upstairs to a certain room, taken to indicate that the occupant had a sleeping companion. Lyon has often been described as *la ville secrète*; and that is certainly the hermetic face that the city has always liked to affect towards strangers. But there cannot have been much secret about life in the rue Neuve or the rue Confort.

Let us now turn our attention to a *voyage à deux* that had some of the characteristics of an abduction—we do not know whether it was followed by pregnancy—and that should have terminated in Marseille, but did in fact end, miserably, in Perrache. On 12 March 1791,

Sr. Jean-Baptiste Ducret, compagnon imprimeur à Lyon, y demeurant, rue Saint-Jean ... employé à l'imprimerie du Sr. Faucheux [déclare] qu'il vient vous dénoncer un rapt de séduction, une action considérée par les loix comme un crime capital. Le Sr. Vagenay, fils du Sr. Vagenay, marchand tripier à la boucherie des Terreaux, a fait la connaissance de Marie Ducret, fille du suppliant. Après avoir tout mis en usage pour la séduire, il a eu recours aux promesses de mariage; âgée de 15 ans et ½ Marie Ducret crut Vagenay; elle consentit de l'épouser mais avec le consentement de son père et de sa mère. Vagenay ... lui persuada qu'il est de leur intérêt respectif de taire ce mariage et qu'il doit être fait secrètement ... Vagenay parvint à l'engager à fuir avec lui à Marseille, l'assurant que c'est là qu'il veut et peut l'épouser. On profite d'un instant où la fille est seule, Vagenay, pour mieux la tromper, lui aide à faire un paquet des hardes dont elle croit avoir besoin; ils s'échappent, les voilà en route. Ils n'allèrent pas loin, la nuit approchoit; ils s'arrêtèrent dans l'allée Perrache à *l'auberge des Deux Amants*; ils y soupèrent; Vagenay présenta la jeune Ducret comme étant sa femme, ils furent accueillis, couchèrent ensemble . . .

Les ayant découverts dans *l'auberge des Deux Amants*, le suppliant y entra accompagné d'une escouade de la garde nationale et des soldats de La Marck . . . on les trouva couchés ensemble . . . Vagenay eut l'adresse de s'évader [what he did was to tell the soldiers that he had to go outside in order to discharge a pressing need, they had let him out, and he had fled through the night, presumably eventually turning up again at home, in les Terreaux] . . . Cette scène affligeante eut lieu le 5 novembre dernier . . . Vagenay père, homme riche, ne veut pas que son fils épouse une fille qui a, selon lui, deux grands défauts, l'une de n'être encore qu'une enfant, l'autre, d'être sans fortune.

It was a wretched ending to a journey that, for the young couple, had started under such excellent auspices, including the inviting roof of an inn so suitably named *l'auberge des deux amants*—and no doubt the name was both an invitation and an indication of the sort of travellers who would be welcomed in an establishment so conveniently placed just beyond the city walls, and on the highroad south. Vagenay probably knew of the place already, as the result of a week-end excursion; or he may have consulted one of his workmates about an accommodating address of this kind, within walking distance of Lyon on a winter's night. He had also shown considerable flair in suggesting to the girl that Marseille would be their chosen Eldorado, that there they would be able to get everything arranged, before coming back to face both lots of parents with the *fait accompli*. A *Lyonnaise* of fifteen would have been aware of Marseille, in a way in which she would not have been aware of Paris, too far away, too foreign ever to have impinged on her imagination. *Marseillais* were familiar figures in eighteenth-century Lyon, the route south was both inviting and facilitated by the Rhône, the principal channel of communication. She would have been prepared to believe that in Marseille there would be no difficulties, no questions asked. Perhaps Vagenay had never intended to go to Marseille at all. But it was the sort of destination to appeal to a teenage girl from Saint-Jean. He may merely have been concerned in getting the girl to bed as quickly as possible, and in a place where they would be likely to escape detection. If this were the case, he must have been singularly inept; for the couple had told several friends and neighbours that they were heading for Marseille, so that the *allée de Perrache* would be the first place anyone would have looked for them, if their departure had been noticed only after nightfall; it was known that they had left on foot, for the parents would have checked, in the first place, with the *bureau des diligences* and the *coche d'eau*. It does then seem that the abductor may have been almost as naïve as the abducted. It was certainly a humiliating end to a trip so full of promise. The night, so brutally interrupted, may have left a more permanent memorial already visible, nearly five months later, in March. If this had not been the case, it is difficult to see why the father should have gone to the trouble and expense of going to court and lodging a formal complaint for abduction against the son of a rich man. For this would hardly have been the best way of persuading Vagenay to allow his son to marry the girl.

As in the matter of *la fille Josèphe*, the episode of the interrupted night, of the young couple caught already in bed, after what must have been an extremely pleasant supper at the inn, is not merely of anecdotal interest. Nor can Marie be seen as a victim; she appears to have been only too willing to be persuaded. The episode is above all yet another reminder of the extent to which aristocratic values and *mores* had penetrated downwards, to permeate even this comparatively humble level of society. For here we have the very classical theme of *l'enlèvement* played out with its principal actors the son of a tripe merchant and the daughter of a companion printer. It is true that here was no closed carriage, no coachman wrapped up to the eyes so that he would not be easily recognised, nor would his livery be visible. At the end of the road, there would be no *pavillon* in the neo-classic manner, its lights faintly seen at the far end of a misty park, its approaches flanked by sphinxes and marine monsters; inside there would be no beautifully adorned bedroom, approached, with a negro page holding up the candles and leading the way, as the lover pressed secret mechanisms that released panels in concealed doors; there would be no superb collation, accompanied by *vins capiteux*, laid out on a Louis XVI side-table, its feet the gilded claws of lions. The young couple would have made their preparations on their own, without the intervention of an army of servants: footmen, coachmen, lady's maids, *bouquetières*. All Vagenay had had to do was to hang about the quartier Saint-Jean, waiting for an opportunity to see the girl on her own, when her parents were out. And, at the end of a road, walked, there would be a carters' inn, probably of no very good repute, and regularly visited by the police. But all these were merely props. In either case, there would be a bed at the end of the journey.

Seduction: masculine language and tactics

In the earlier stages of a developing relationship between a young man and a girl of much the same age and condition, and living in the same city, sometimes, as we have seen, both strangers there, having come from the same village, or originating from the same quarter, or contiguous quarters, the language and tactics likely to be followed, in a series of prudent and searching moves, by both parties, will generally follow an almost conventional, formalised pattern, a sort of moral *gavotte*, the steps of which bring the partners now so close, as almost to be touching, now distant from each other, feigning indifference or slights, a dance that in fact, though stepped out in the tender or mocking intimacy of *à deux*, would never be lacking an appreciative, critical or disapproving audience, there primarily to see that the rules were observed by both sides. For in the conditions of eighteenth-century Lyon, the only thing of which one could be quite certain would be that such tentative gropings would be watched by large numbers of people : workmates, brothers, sisters, room-mates—and the presence of these might at an early stage prove a valuable insurance, though, later, it would be necessary to persuade him or her to go—employers, and, indeed, employees, neighbours, much of the street, the idlers and *badauds* on the quays, *sur la Promenade*, on the *cours*, place Bellecour, in the marshy woodlands and scrub of les Brotteaux, in the *guinguettes* of la Guillotière, or those high up on the two hills : Fourvière and Saint-Just, and la Croix-Rousse. For, in Lyon, there is an established geography of leisure, of walking, idling, gaping, and wild jigging and frenetic dancing, so often the point of departure, the opening of the Tunnel of Love, before the rattling train disappears into the screaming, dusty darkness, with its characteristic smell of dust and gun-powder. And perhaps the fairground is no bad metaphor for an exercise closely governed by leisure, by the open spaces, and by feast days, week-ends, and festivals. It would be as easy to draw up, from the evidence of the girls' statements, an urban or 'faubourienne' *carte du tendre*, as it would be to illustrate the distribution through the city of *ateliers* and *entrepôts*. In short, seduction would be as formalised at this level of society as it was in Valmont's protracted tactics to bring down the prudish and virtuous *Présidente*.

It will follow a predictable pattern, imposed by collective conventions and unstated assumptions, the collective honour of a family, the fear of parental disapproval, the solidarity of workmates, of those who follow a similar trade, a moral solidarity, based on friendship and mutual preservation, rather than an embryonic trade union, the opinions and prejudices of neighbours, the observations of those who live on the same storey, and who watch every time a door is opened, and of those whom one passes on the stairs, late at night or early in the morning. The receipt of a letter, then read out loud *en petit comité*, by a literate friend or workmate, thus becomes a pledge, almost as binding as a formal demand to parents. A regular visit to a girl on Sundays or feast days has a similar force of promise, especially if the girl, when the man, for some good reason, is unable to come, stays alone in her room all Sunday.[1] *Demander l'entrée de la maison* is of course an even more traditional pledge on the future, both in urban and rural communities; and to go back on it would be a severe assault on popular morality. Even to be seen regularly on *la Promenade*, on the arm of a young man, but accompanied too by one's friends and mates of both sexes, is considered as a form of pledge, perhaps not entirely binding, but none the less a clear statement of intention; and the larger the number of witnesses, of those who have gone out together with the couple, the more powerful will be the message for the future. To take a girl out to eat *chez un traiteur*, to display her thus to the public of the long tables, at which are seated people who will almost certainly know both the girl and her host, is also a step towards formalising a relationship. Sometimes the *traiteur* himself will step forward to congratulate the couple, or, equally, to banter with them on their good fortune, with crude allusions to future joys, the whole thing played out to a loud, appreciative and guffawing audience, coarse, but not unkindly. Needless to say, there may also be the more formal, clearly-stated bid on the future, the *promesse de mariage*.

The run-up to seduction will take different forms in different places. Much depends on geography and climate. In Paris it is likely to be a more secretive and intimate affair than in Lyon, where each stage, save the ultimate one, will generally be played out in the open, in the street, in the tavern, in the wide empty space offered by the quays, by a huge square, the monument to the conceit of monarchs, but used appreciatively by those with very different, homelier aspirations. It will be a sunny business, as full of light and airiness as one of Goya's colourful and dusty fair scenes in eighteenth-century Madrid. So *la gavotte* will be closely related to the principal compensation, one would be tempted to say, wealth, of the poor of both sexes, the freedom of the street, the escape from dark, miasmic *cours* and cellars, from fifth-storey rooms containing five or six mattresses, from the sweat and heat of the *atelier*, from the acrid smell of raw silk, feathers and stuffs, from the steaming humidity of the laundry, from the noisy ground-floor forge of a *maréchal* and the terrible stink of a *triperie* off les Terreaux.

The *déclarations* often seem to suggest bright sunlight, open spaces,

---

[1] André Charpenet, a witness for Marguerite Gulon, 'matelassier, à Lyon, y demeurant place Saint-Georges...39 ans...nous observe seulement qu'allant fréquemment voir quelqu'un qui demeure dans le même corps de logis que la plaignante, il a eu occasion de rencontrer le nommé Bonhomme avec la plaignante.' Another witness, Anne Coilier, *brodeuse*, rue de la Ruelle-Renversée, aged 24½, states 'qu'elle demeure porte à porte avec la plaignante...elle a vu fréquemment et presque tous les jours le Sr. Bonhomme chez le plaignante, qu'ils alloient souvent à la promenade ensemble, que quand il ne venait pas la chercher le dimanche, elle ne sortoit pas de son domicile.'

the yellowy dust of the *Promenade* blown to and fro in a gusty southern wind, the dark shadows thrown by the tall façades of the rue Mercière, the rue Bouteille, the rue Terraille and the rue Sainte-Catherine as it creeps timidly uphill, a study of ochre, deep black, brilliant blue, with stems of tender green peeping over grey-yellow walls on the *montées*, the alarming, tumultuous greenish-grey of the Rhône, a river without the least hint of amiability, offering no invitation to dawdle, to bathe, or to wash out clothing (though this might be done in some of its calmer, more pacific pools, among the sand-banks near the porte de Saint-Clair), and not even an attraction to fishermen, merely a permanent threat and a visible frontier. No wonder 'la Guille' and les Brotteaux enjoyed such a detestable reputation with Lyonnais and Lyonnaises, especially the latter, of all conditions. They would think of them as others might refer to 'outre-Rhin', 'outre-Quiévrain', or 'outre-Manche'. La Guillotière was not a safe place for innocent girls; and we will encounter one whose downfall dated from a week-end christening party held there. It was perhaps the first time that she had crossed the river. And even at this period, the bridges; pont de la Boucle, pont de la porte Saint-Clair, pont de la Guillotière, form the no-man's land between the relative safety and predictability of the central quarters, and the sinister marsh-lands beyond, the terrain of duels and casual murders, long before the conditions created by terror and repression had made them the favoured killing grounds of the White Terror.[1] Perhaps it is not mere chance that so many of our *déclarations*—over two-thirds of them, made between five and eight and a half months from conception—should have dated from the winter months, and especially from November, December, January and February, visible and unwelcome reminders of happy spring excursions, of summer walks and explorations, among the hills or in the woodlands and sand-banks on the other side of the Rhône, of warm nights along the quays. The spring and summer would count among the poor girl's inalienable luxuries. But the memory of them would be doubly bitter when carrying a winter stomach.

Indeed, what the statements reveal most strikingly with the passage of time, as the date of lying-in approaches inexorably, is an increasing and fundamental difference in the very definition of time itself. For the girl, six or seven months gone, too late for the intervention of a *faiseuse d'ange*, even assuming that she had ever been able to hear of the existence of one through one of her older female employers, or from another *brodeuse*, time is running out. The future can be counted in weeks, and the often-promised marriage becomes more and more imperative : 'Let us decide on a date.' But for the man, the future above all is not thus boldly to be defined, pinned down to a fixed date; it must be endlessly and

[1] See ch. 2 of my *Reactions to the French Revolution* (London, 1972).

vaguely extendable, best expressed in that conveniently vague and much-used adverb *incessamment*, which may mean anything; it will always be just round the corner, just out of sight, a desperate bid to gain time, a little more time, in the hope that something will turn up, that an escape route will suddenly present itself, that a second seducer will be discovered, even that a man ready to take on a pregnant girl may be found. When it is not *incessament*, then it is the old calendar, the old feast days, always safely away in the future. If it is November, there will not be much harm in saying 'on se mariera à Pâques'; if it is April, 'on se mariera à la Trinité' will still give plenty of time. There are any number of excuses to be found to justify an ever-later date: parents to be consulted, financial arrangements to be made, a necessary journey first to be gone on, lodgings to be found, furniture to be acquired, a mattress to be paid for, money to be borrowed, a place in the country, *en nourrice*, to be secured. Thus time can only increase the fundamental divergence that may have started, on the part of both participants, in affection, tenderness, friendship, and thoughtlessness, especially about the future. Now, as acidity begins to corrode the relationship, the girl's insistence on the subject of the future will become increasingly strident and unwelcome; the weaker, more easy-going man will attempt to keep away, the more brutal one may take to blows. Whatever her previous weaknesses or even encouragements, the girl will now harp on her innocence and naïveté. It had all been a calculated piece of masculine villainy, a sort of reasoned *escroquerie sur l'avenir* calculated, from the very start, to break down the girl's defences, and give preferably rapid satisfaction to masculine lust. But, in some of the cases quoted, we hear of couples who have known each other, *se fréquentant*, in the innocent sense of going out together, spending their leisure together, as much as six or ten years. In retrospect, when the girl makes her *déclaration*, she will see this long time-lag as an additional manifestation of masculine calculation and selfishness, the sinister tactics of a Fabius, the cruel deliberation of a person who, for years and years, has dealt out kind words, kisses, and warm smiles, concealing, all the time, his fell purpose. Yet, how often could this delay have in fact pleaded in the man's favour, suggesting the solidity of his affections and the seriousness of his purpose? They must not rush headlong into marriage; but must wait till, economically, they are both reasonably well set up. And then all such deeply laid plans can be undermined in the course of a summer night. The girls *have* to put all the blame on the men, *have* to argue convincingly that they have been seduced, as many, but by no means all, undoubtedly have. It does not really matter to us whether they have, or have not been. We are not the judges who received these statements and who had to try to decide whether there was a convincing case for a paternity order.

But we must constantly bear in mind this widening divergence of interest between male and female, if we are correctly to interpret these documents, and to attempt to reach behind the girl's version of the story, of necessity designed to suggest that it has been the man who, from start to finish, has made all the running, and that she has merely been over-trusting, candid, and innocent. We should not make too much of these professions of candour, for even the most ignorant *brodeuse* will have had impressed upon her, from childhood, both by her parents, and in church, the moral and economic value of virginity. Indeed, the reluctance of many of these girls to face their families is a clear indication that, in most cases, the lesson had made a deep imprint.

There are other assumptions that we may safely make, without attempting to press our material too far, to make it testify for what it in fact conceals or leaves vague. In the master-servant context, indeed, in the employer-employee one, it is reasonable to assume that the man's intentions are entirely dishonourable, especially when he is already married. But it does not follow that, for instance, the servant has been all that wide-eyed and defenceless. The female domestic of a rich man did not have to have read Swift to have seen her opportunity, especially if with child, to set her cap, if not at the master (the father of the child), then at least, in a rich house, at his steward.[1] Masters had, it is true, what might be described as the advantages of *les lieux*, that is, of the choice of the most propitious time and place. He could call the girl down to the cellar to help him with the wine; or he could ask her to accompany him to his place in the country, in the Monts du Lyonnais or the Beaujolais, to do some washing. Any girl who ventured into such dangerous places would have been asking for trouble. It is also reasonable to suppose that a girl who accuses a man ten years younger than herself may be using her condition in an attempt to secure herself a husband. This is of course what young men thus accused would be the first to claim. Finally, some of the girls may indeed have been as easy conquests as their alleged seducers were likely to suggest. There was probably not much to be said for girls who picked up with soldiers, medical students, or *garçons perruquiers*, whereas a *brodeuse* who had been seduced by a man in the same trade might indeed have been as innocent and trusting as both she herself and her workmates, sometimes too her female employer, *marchande brodeuse*, *marchande chapelière*, were to come forward and affirm.

---

[1] In such a family, if you are handsome, you will have the choice of three lovers; the chaplain, the steward, and my lord's gentleman. I would first advise you to chuse the steward; but if you happen to be young with child by my lord, you must take up with the chaplain. I like my lord's gentleman the least of the three, for he is usually vain and saucy from the time he throws off his livery; and if he misseth a pair of colours, or a tide-waiter's place, he hath no remedy but the highway. (Swift, 'Directions to the *Waiting-maid*'.)

There is even the case of a *marchande* being witnessed for by one of her *apprenties,* though the testimony of the latter may not have been entirely voluntary and disinterested. Clearly, within a trade, there exist unstated rules of the game, and when these have been infringed, there will be a general rallying-round the aggrieved party, even on the part of masculine workmates and neighbours.

Perhaps there is no need to labour any of these points further, as we have already heard a number of detailed versions offered by the girls and have been made insistently aware of the importance of the *promesse de mariage*, preferably at a named season, as an inducement to compliance with masculine demands. At this stage it would perhaps be best to allow some of the girls to tell their own stories, in their own words, or, rather, in the rather formalised and much more educated and reasoned words put in their mouths by judge or *greffier*, who took down their statements and who tended to standardise them into set formulae that lend to the loss of virginity and the beginnings of pregnancy, both events of tragic proportions to the victim, much of the banality and inhumanity of the language of French law. After reading fifty or more of these statements, the historian has to remind himself that this was not an inventory of stock in a bankruptcy suit, nor the dull litany of objects read out in a sing-song voice by a *notaire* at the drawing up of a marriage contract, but a statement revealing the most intimate, and often tragic, aspects of a girl's present and bleak immediate future, and that *la comparante, la déposante, la plaignante,* or whatever other semi-neutered description she was arbitrarily placed under disguised the reality of the living, and often no doubt attractive and appetising Pernon, Thérèse, Françoise, Marianne, Annette, Gasparde, Suzanne, Virginie, Benoîte, Louise, Jeanne, Marthe (signed *Marte*), Pierrette, Catherine, Isabelle, Marguerite, Claudine, Antoinette, Martine, Constantine, Denise, Barbe, Philippe, *Lyonnaises,* or girls from the region, who had been given these names by their parents or guardians, or by the parish priest. Nor, when describing a decision that would account for her presence before the judge, would the girl herself have said that 'elle lui accorda les dernières faveurs', 'elle céda à ses instances pressantes', 'elle porte aujourd' hui les marques visibles de cet excès de confiance', and so on and so forth. What the girl herself would have said would have been expressed in terms more direct, cruder, and less circumlocutory. The language of the law is so disguised. so allusive, that, at times, one is liable to forget what these statements are in fact about. It is true that eighteenth-century language, possibly even at this level, often affects an indirect and metaphorical approach to this ancient and oft-described activity, and that Cleland succeeds in describing the act a hundred or more times without ever using the word 'copulation'. But we should make allowances for the pithy directness of popular language; and it does not seem probable that a *Lyonnaise* would be anv less inclined to call a spade a spade than a *dame de la Halle*, from Paris.

It would then be appropriate, at this stage, to begin with the most familiar, commonest theme of master-servant, or employer-employee seduction, for this was the easiest form of seduction to carry out, as it placed the man from the outset in a position of tremendous strength, and the girl at a complete disadvantage, both at the time, and later. when, so often, it would be her word against that of her former master. who had the advantage of being able to prove his case by the mere fact of dismissal. A domestic servant who had been dismissed must be presumed to have 'mené une mauvaise vie'. The unequal relationship is generally emphasised in the girls' own statements, in the standard expression : 'profitant de l'ascendant qu'il avait sur moi', 'le Sr. Tamisier a profité de l'ascendant qu'un maître a sur ses ouvriers', or, in this case, referring to the master's son, always as much a threat as the master himself : 'le Sr. Jean-Marie Peclet, son fils, voulut abuser de l'ascendant que sa qualité lui donnoit sur elle pour la séduire.' Indeed many masters seem to think that to seduce their servants was not merely an opportunity, but a right. For instance here is the case of Françoise Baroud, 'demeurante à Lyon, rue de l'Enfant-qui-pisse,' who states :

> ... que sur la fin de l'année 1789 la plaignante entra en qualité de domestique chez le Sr. Ferrand, marchand culottier... à peine deux mois, furent-ils expirés qu'il reconnut quelques bonnes qualités dans la plaignante & lui proposa de l'épouser.
>
> Cette dernière, qu'un avenir heureux flattoit, consentit volontiers à cet engagement... aussitôt qu'elle s'est aperçue enceinte, elle en a fait part à son ravisseur, qui, voulant cacher sa conduite, s'éloigna de son domicile au mois de juillet dernier.

In January 1791, she is eight months pregnant.

The master, Jacques Ferrand, forty-three, *marchand culottier, en peau*, rue Puits du sel, questioned by the judge,

> répond qu'elle a été à son service, mais qu'il l'a mise hors de chez lui il y a environ 10 mois, parce qu'il s'est aperçu qu'elle menait une mauvaise vie.
>
> A lui représenté que la mauvaise vie qu'a pu mener cette fille n'excuserait pas lui répondant d'avoir eu un mauvais commerce avec elle... Répond que cette fille demeurant chez lui en qualité de Domestique, il n'a eu d'autre rapport avec elle que le service qu'elle faisait dans son ménage.
>
> Interpellé de convenir que les rapports qu'il a eus avec cette fille ne sont pas seulement ceux d'un maître avec son domestique, qu'il est accusé d'avoir fait avec elle des parties de plaisir qui annonçoient une liaison plus suspecte, qu'il l'a menée dans des cabarets, qu'il y a demandé une chambre en particulier, qu'il y a mangé avec elle, et qu'ils paraissaient tellement familiers

que le maître du cabaret demanda à cette fille si lui répondant étoit son amoureux.

Répond et dénie tout le contenu.

But the judge, well used to the professional *morgue* of masters, when accused of having misused one of their servants, would have none of this:

A lui demandé si lors du temps de la fédération, il n'a pas été plusieurs fois se promener avec la plaignante dans l'enceinte dud. Camp [Even the Revolution could thus serve the very private designs of lovers and seducers!] Répond . . . qu'il n'est jamais allé se promener avec elle.

Ferrand decided to take legal advice. He further insinuated that, before entering his service, Françoise had already had at least one child and several lovers, and that she was attempting to wreak vengeance on him for having sacked her. In order to clinch his argument, he added the detail that during the period in question, he could not have had sexual relations with the girl, 'étant malade et n'étant pas capable de copulation'. Perhaps he was overdoing it, for he was unable to produce a medical certificate to this effect. Anyhow, another witness seems to have been of a very different opinion. François Dumas, *compagnon cordonnier*, twenty-six,

dépose que le 15 ou 16 juin dernier [1790], allant porter une paire de souliers à François Baroud . . . il entra dans la boutique . . . n'y ayant trouvé personne, il pénétra plus avant et dans une espèce de cabinet à main droite il vit la plaignante et le Sr. Ferrand sur un lit étant dans led. cabinet, que ce dernier descendit aussitôt dud. lit et remit sa culotte qui était à bas.

Ferrand had evidently recovered his powers. It might be emphasised, too, that with the constant to-ing and fro-ing that are necessary accompaniments and indeed one of the principal consolations of life in a pre-industrial urban society, seduction during working hours was relatively easy and was no doubt as often observed by the unexpected visitor or intruder.

A further witness, Claudine Péronnat, aged thirty,

dépose qu'aux environs de la Saint-Jean dernier, restant pour lors rue Pierre-Scise et près la rue Puits du sel, passant au-devant de la boutique du Sr. Ferrand . . . sur environ 9 heures du soir, elle vit led. Sr. Ferrand qui embrassait la plaignante, et avait avec elle des familiarités qui fixèrent l'attention de plusieurs personnes qui passaient dans la rue au-devant de la boutique.

Lyon, if not strictly speaking a southern town, either in language, more akin to *dauphinois*, or in *mores*, in the sense of the extended family, the tribalism and violence of *les méridionaux,* and of southern brutality where children were concerned, was, like Marseille, a city in which the street, as much as *Guignol* himself, constituted a sort of open, permanent and free theatre for the benefit of the passer-by, with the best perform-ances scheduled for the evening hours, when the windows were wide open to capture a little of the cool creeping in from the Rhône or from the Monts du Lyonnais, and when there would be plenty of people, couples, families, lonely *voyeurs, badauds,* out and about, in search of free entertainment : a drunken brawl, a shouting match between two women, a fracas outside a *cabaret,* or, perhaps, best of all, the spectacle so generously and regularly offered, rue Confort, by a *marchande fripière* whose odyssey will concern us later. This is why in Lyon 'the freedom of the street' would probably be more valued than in Paris, a city in which one would perhaps be disinclined to dawdle. *Entre Rhône et Saône,* with its tall, narrow streets trapping the heat, would force people out of doors, towards the windy quays of the Rhône, towards the pont la Feuillée, to watch the east-west traffic. And Lyon had a double bonus, possessing two rivers, rather than one.

Similar to the experience of François Baroud, though it concerns the relationship between employer and employee in silk manufacture, and not that between master and domestic, is that of Marie Perrichon, *dévideuse de soie, demeurant rue Saint-Georges,*

procédante à cause de sa minorité de l'autorité de Philippe Perrichon, son père, compagnon maçon à Neuville...que le 15 avril 1791, âgée de 18 ans, elle entra au service du Sr. Quet, marchand fabricant d'étoffes de soie... place de la Croix-Paquet, en qualité de devideuse. Celui, âgé d'environ 50 ans, et marié, commença par alléguer le poids des services qu'il devait attendre de son ouvrière; il eut pour elle sur les autres certains égards, certaine préférence en toutes choses; bientôt elle s'attacha naïvement aux intérêts et à la personne de son maître, sans soupçonner qu'il avoit des vues criminelles...de coutume, c'est Quet qui va chercher dans sa cave le vin et quelques autres denrées dont son ménage a besoin. Cet endroit est extrêmement sombre, il est impossible d'y pénétrer sans une lumière, sous le prétexte de la lui porter...Quet y invita une première fois la plaignante, qui obéit. Là il commença la séduction par des promesses de bien-être, il la caressa et se permit même des licences qui cependant n'attaquaient point la pudeur.

But this was merely the softening-up process :

La plaignante succomba et ce commerce charnel dura 3 mois et $\frac{1}{2}$ consécutifs pendant 4 et $\frac{1}{2}$ qu'elle est restée dans la maison dont elle ne sortit que lorsqu'elle fut convaincue qu'elle était enceinte.

Such an extreme disproportion between the ages of master and servant, employer and employee, is characteristic of eighteenth-century urban

society, when it would be common for a girl barely nubile to be in the
service of a master already middle-aged. Much of the sexual attraction
of domestic servants to their masters and employers can certainly be
attributed to the fact that they were both so young and so inexperienced
(or, better still, *apparently* inexperienced, for it is the uncertainty that
arouses the man well advanced in life). Quet was a married man of
fifty, his wife was probably not very much younger, and the master may
have hinted to his employee, in the course of the sessions in the cellar,
at the possibility of a divorce, for the new Codes had by then been
introduced. The possibility of exchanging places legally, as well as
physically, with the master's wife may have been a powerful inducement
to Marie to comply with Quet's desires. Such great reversals of fortune
did in fact happen, as Swift reminds us.

Quet, like most people, had a cellar. The next seducer, in the master-
servant category, had a house in the country, a convenient base, especially for a married man, from which to operate a discreet seduction, the
bourgeois equivalent of Valmont's use of his country *château*, and of
the *château* season, to further his designs on *la Présidente* :

> Françoise André, native de la paroisse de Montluel, fille domestique ci-devant
> au service du Sr. Charrettier, aubergiste, rue de Trion, demeurant actuelle-
> ment chez la veuve Mathéra, garde-malade, rue de la Barre . . . [dépose] qu'elle
> a demeuré au service du Sr. Charrettier pendant 22 mois, dans les derniers
> tems le Sr. Charrettier, qui avait conçu le dessein de la séduire, sous le pré-
> texte de lui aider à faire une lessive dans une maison de campagne à la Tour-
> de-Salvagny où il étoit pour lors, lui fit l'ordre d'aller l'y rejoindre.

This is perhaps the crudest example of masculine lust in our collection.
No compliments, no promises, no efforts to impress the poor girl, no
drawing aside of the curtain of the future to reveal the marriage bed,
le bonheur, or a journey to a distant part of the kingdom, no dinner *en
tête à tête*, no *partie fine*, no *promenade*, just an order. Domestic servants, especially those of innkeepers, are mere *bêtes à séduction*; they
do not even merit the dubious effort of 'chatting up', they are ordered
into bed, or whatever it may be, as they are ordered to wash the floor,
clean out the kitchen, or do the week's washing. If Françoise had refused
to report for duty at La Tour-de-Salvagny—where her employer had
presumably gone to be unobserved by his wife—she would have been
sacked. So she went, and was sacked anyway.[1]

---

[1] It would hardly be an exaggeration to suggest that eighteenth-century female
domestics often lived in a veritable terror of their masters, not merely because there
was always the danger of seduction, but because they feared that they might be
dismissed for some trivial failure: oversleeping, failure to respond immediately to
the imperious summons of a bell, a breakage. There is a pathetic example from Paris
of the atmosphere of terror in which a young girl in service, especially if recently

It may be presumed that female domestics had fewer illusions than *brodeuses* or others in the silk trade, for, when not subjected to the assiduities of *le fils du patron*, they would be at the disposition of innkeepers, perhaps even of their customers, their anatomy would have been much commented on by drinkers, as, *filles de salle*, they bent down, washing the floor; they might, before ultimate degradation, have passed through many hands, and received few expressions of friendship or affection. And in large establishments, the houses of the rich, the *hôtels particuliers* of the *soyeurs* of Ainay, they would be further exposed to the predatory assaults of male domestics, *la valetaille,* dressed in the master's discarded clothes, and adopting the young master's cavalier attitudes to women. A footman, perhaps more than anyone, would be anxious to assert his position below stairs by seducing the kitchen maid. But girls in other occupations appear to have few illusions about what to expect from a manservant.

> Philippe Montagne, devideuse de soie à Lyon ... Petite rue Thomassin ... [dépose] qu'elle est enceinte de près de 9 mois des oeuvres du nommé Cortey, domestique, et qu'elle a pris des arrangements avec l'hôpital général de la charité pour y placer l'enfant dont elle doit accoucher.

And that is that, and quite right too; for she cannot even give the man a Christian name.

Jeanne Coton has moved from domestic service to the trade of *dévideuse,* 'dans la maison du Sr. Chatard, rue Pareille, quartier ...

---

taken on, might be living. The *commissaire de police* of the Section de la Butte des Moulins, the quarter of the Palais-Royal, received a statement from a girl's employer, Jacques Geoffroy, *peintre doreur*, who came to report, on 4 Frimaire Year III (25 November 1795) that the girl had been discovered unconscious in the courtyard of his house, rue des Moulins, after falling out of the window of her attic room:

> que Marie-Anne Lâche était sa fille de confiance depuis 3 jours et que les deux premiers jours qu'elle a été chez lui, s'est levée longtems avant le jour et est venue sonner & frapper à sa porte pour demander ce qu'elle avait à faire, et qu'il lui répondit qu'il falloit qu'elle se couchât, qu'il n'était pas tems de se lever, qu'il croit que cette fille avait toujours peur de ne pas faire son devoir, car elle s'est levée toutes les nuits qu'elle est chez lui, qu'elle était seule dans sa chambre.

The doctor believed that she must have fallen out of the window in her sleep. Fortunately, she got away with nothing worse than a broken leg, though even that would be a major disaster for a serving maid, as it would incapacitate her for a time at least. Questioned at the Hôtel Dieu, she could not remember how she had come to fall (*A.P.P.* A/A 95, commissaire de police de la Section de la Butte des Moulins, procès-verbal en date du 4 frimaire an III). The extent of the girl's anxiety is a terrifying reminder of the extreme fragility of the status of a female domestic in eighteenth-century urban society. Dismissal would be a constant threat; and, after dismissal, what then? Prostitution, the humiliation of a return home, exposure to cold, starvation, or employment in some even more wretched capacity, such as laundress or *marchande de fagots*. Domestics, after all, were at least housed and, above all *fed*, and sometimes even *clothed*.

Saint-Vincent'. She explains the reasons for this change of occupation:

Il y a environ 6 années qu'elle est entrée au service du Sr. Jean Peclet, bourgeois de cette ville, demeurant sur le quai Saint-Vincent [she has not moved away very far, no doubt to the annoyance of the Peclet family, remaining in the parish, near the houses of the wealthy inhabitants of this quay of the Saône], elle ne fut pas plus tôt dans cette maison que le Sr. Jean-Marie Peclet, son fils, voulut abuser de l'ascendant que sa qualité donnoit sur elle pour la séduire, après 18 mois elle quitta le service du Sr. Peclet et ne fut pas pour cela délivrée des sollicitations du Sr. Jean-Marie Peclet qui n'en fut que plus assidu auprès de la remontrante qui est devenue *deux fois* enceinte, elle a d'abord fait un garçon qui n'a vécu que 11 mois, elle en a fait un autre qui est âgé de 19 mois, elle est en ce moment enceinte pour la *troisième fois*, toujours des oeuvres du Sr. Jean-Marie Peclet, de plus de 8 mois et ½ ... Le Sr. Peclet vient, par un procédé atroce, d'abandonner la remontrante sans secours, sans moyens de fournir à ses besoins à l'instant d'accoucher.

Jeanne produces a witness, presumably a workmate, and judging from her address, either her room-mate as well, or living in the same lodging-house:

Marie Besson, dévideuse de soie ... rue Pareille ... 27 ans ... [dépose] qu'à une de ces époques elle vit led. Sr. Peclet sortir de table, qu'elle comprit qu'il avait dîné avec la plaignante, parce qu'il y avoit encore deux couverts sur la table.

A second witness, also a *dévideuse*, and giving the same address, is equally observant—and equally damning: 'Il y a environ 2 mois elle vit entrer le Sr. Peclet chez la plaignante, et que led. Sr. Peclet avait un paquet sous le bras.' The implication presumably being that the parcel contained some of his clothing, and that he was going to spend the night, or, equally, that he had recognised his paternal responsibilities, and was bringing clothing for the surviving boy. What seems established is his insistence in pursuing the girl, years after her departure from his parents' home.

What is equally apparent is her determination—and who can blame her, with a third pregnancy at the hands of Peclet—not to let matters rest; and in this respect, her attitude is much in contrast to the humble resignation and fatalism of most of the *déclarantes*. For she produces a third witness—she must have drummed up pretty well all the girls on her storey—also from the rue Pareille, describing herself as 'une ouvrière en étoffes de soie, âgée de 30 ans', who states that 'comme la fenêtre de sa chambre donnait sur l'escalier, elle voyoit monter fréquemment le Sr. Jean-Marie Peclet fils'.

He was indeed closely observed, and no doubt much commented upon by these girls, no longer young, by eighteenth-century standards—and

Jeanne herself must have been nearing thirty, as she had known Peclet for over six years—and thus probably more aware than most that time was running out for their companion as far as marriage prospects were concerned. Peclet too gives his age as twenty-eight. The judge clearly thought the case unusually important, for he took some trouble to question him closely, making much of the meal or meals that they had had together, and asking him why he had been seen coming *out* of the house with a parcel under his arm. (The witness had said that she had seen him coming *in* with it, a less damaging assertion, because if he still had it on leaving, it would have been clear that he had spent the night in Jeanne's room.) Peclet denied everything, or as much as he could, replying

> qu'il a été attiré dans le domicile de cette fille par des parents de cette dernière pour faire un arangement sur l'accusation qu'on méditait de porter contre lui, qu'à cette époque il a en effet mange chez cette fille avec lesdits parents, et en est sorti avec eux sans faire aucun arrangement, n'étant point l'auteur de la grossesse.

His denial of responsibility, underlined by his sneering reference to Jeanne as *cette fille*, is entirely predictable on the part of a *fils de famille* who lived on the affluent Quai Saint-Vincent, the principal base of the *notariat* of Lyon. The girl was being a persistent nuisance, insisting on haunting the quarter, wandering around displaying her stomach. Peclet's story about being trapped into accepting a meal, in order to meet her family—and this is the only time that we hear of Jeanne's relatives—is hardly convincing. At least, none of the witnesses could remember having seen any other visitors coming in or going out of the girl's room. Of course, it is just possible that Jeanne was telling a pack of lies, for Peclet's son would have been a good catch for a former servant who was only a *dévideuse*. Her female neighbours and workmates would have been likely to stand by her in any case, through thick and thin. But it seems much more likely that Peclet *fils* was unable to break with her entirely.

The abuse of the position of master or employer was obviously the commonest instrument of seduction, in a society in which domestic servants would constitute fifteen per cent of the feminine labour force in most cities (this was the figure for Paris at this time; for Toulouse it was a little lower, twelve per cent), and in which, in Lyon, *brodeuses*, *dévideuses* and so on would have accounted for as much as twenty-five per cent. This was simply a matter of exploiting a position of total power. But there was a more sophisticated, less naked approach that seems to have been used by the potential seducer and to have been accepted as a point in his favour by a number of girls : the insistence on the similarity of age and condition. Benoîte Bonnard had thought that she could eventually count on Pierre Dusurgey, it will be recalled, because they were both much of an age, and both worked in the hat trade, she as a *coupeuse de poils*, he as a *compagnon chapelier*. Marie Pierry, too, had listened favourably to the pleas of Louis Guichon, because 'la plaignante, jeune et sans expérience, devait compter sur ce mariage, puisque Louis Guichon est un jardinier dont la fortune n'est pas au-dessus de la sienne'. In this case, there was a triple tie, because, while the girl lived in Villeurbanne, the gardener lived nearby, montée de Balmont. Jeanne Caillot, 'brodeuse à Lyon, demeurant rue Plat-d'Argent, âgée de 30 ans', states similarly

> qu'il y a nombre d'années que le commerce de broderies a amené dans son domicile le Sr. Claude-Marie Desvernai, commis chez le Sr. Sonnet, marchand brodeur . . . led. Desvernai a depuis longtems proposé à la comparante de l'épouser, comme l'état et l'âge de ce dernier, qui est âgé de 40 ans, étaient très sortables, la comparante a cru aux promesses dud. Desvernai . . . le Sr. Desvernai, loin de tenir sa parole, s'est absenté.

Equally, Marie Madeleine Martin, *faiseuse de bourses de cheveux*, aged twenty-two, rue des Missionnaires, was to explain

> que depuis 5 ans le Sr. André Colombet, maître ferblantier, lui rend des soins assidus, que depuis ce tems il a parlé souvent à la comparante du dessein où il était de l'épouser, la comformité d'état et d'âge, led. Sr. Colombet ayant environ 26 ans, a fait croire à la comparante que les promesses . . . étoient sincères, elle a cédé . . . le Sr. Colombet paraît avoir des motifs pour éloigner de quelque tems leur union . . . comme le sort de l'enfant dont elle est enciente lui est cher.

In both these cases, the sheer length of the relationship—in the former, several years, in the latter, they had known one another for five years—must have seemed to the two girls a further guarantee of the men's serious intentions, though, reading these statements, one often has occasion to be surprised by the number of girls who claim to have been made pregnant by men whom they had known and with whom they had been going out for anything up to the last ten or eleven years.[1] It is difficult to know what we should make of this. In some cases, it might have been that the couple had decided on a long engagement to enable them to save up enough to set themselves up in an establishment,

---

[1] 'Marthe Villard, tailleuse à Lyon, demeurant rue Saint-Pierre-le-Vieux . . . 19 ans . . . [déclare] qu'il y a 6 ans qu'elle fit la connaissance du nommé Simon Picard, domestique de la veuve Ferrier.' If we are to believe her, Ferrier must have met her when she was only thirteen. Perhaps they had been childhood friends; or perhaps he was merely a skilled exponent of the waiting game.

and that their calculations had been thrown out of joint by an unexpected and unwelcome pregnancy that had caused the man to think
again. For, a woman of thirty and a man of forty can hardly have been
sexually inexperienced, and such long periods of voluntary abstention
seem extremely improbable. This is, however, not the sort of thing that
is likely to be revealed by a *déclaration de grossesse.* Another, less charit-
able explanation might be that the girls mentioned, having become pregnant as the result of other contacts, had fallen back on long-standing
men friends, in the hope that they would regularise the situation.

Just as age, trade, quarter and contiguity may prove to be valuable
allies of seduction, so can certain days, certain occasions, certain periods
of the year, and certain places favour such enterprises. The rôle of
physical proximity (*voisinage*) is an obvious one, for, in any relationship
between male and female, there has to be a starting point : where to
meet? And how to meet? There is a statement, for instance, to the
commissaire de police of the Section Popincourt, in Paris, that spells this
out very clearly :

La citoyenne Nicole Moricard, âgée de 25 ans, demeurant à Paris, cul de sac
Sébastien No 2, fille de Edme Moricard et de femme Françoise Palois, de la
paroisse de Sauvigny-le-Bois [near Avallon], demeurante à Paris depuis environ
4 ans ... pendant près de 3 ans elle a travaillé en qualité de journalière chez
de C. Driancourt, jardinier, rue Popincourt ... pendant tout ce tems, et avant,
elle a vécu d'une manière irréprochable [we have her word for it] ... à la
sollicitation du C. Nicolas Langrand, alors porteur d'eau, et actuellement
voiturier sur le port, *demeurant cul de sac Sébastien No 2*, elle a été demeurer
chez lui le 1er janvier 1794, et que pour l'engager d'y entrer, il lui offrit
moitié plus de gages qu'elle ne gagnoit chez le C. Driancourt, ce qui l'a
déterminé d'y entrer ... à l'époque de cette entrée l'épouse du C. Langrand
existoit et est depuis décédée ... pendant l'espace de 5 mois après la mort de
son épouse, il s'est comporté en galant homme ... quelque tems après il a
commencé à faire des propositions ... il couchait dans une chambre servant
de cuisine & ladite citoyenne ... dans l'écurie, au bout de lad. chambre com-
muniquant dans la surd. écurie ... [il] a eu le premier de la déclarante ...
[elle est] enceinte de 8 mois et de quelques jours.[1]

All one can say is that the country girl, employed in a country trade
in Paris—the Section Popincourt had a great many gardens—and coming
from the same part of the world as Restif's *la paysanne*, seems to have
gone into this with her eyes open. Perhaps she thought that the presence
of Langrand's wife offered a guarantee of her virtue, as indeed it seems
to have done. But she was surely asking for trouble, staying on in her
stable room, after the wife had died. Or perhaps she had calculated that

[1] *Archives de la Préfecture de Police* A/A 219 (commissaire de police de la Section
Popincourt, déclaration faite par Nicole Moricard, le 22 ventôse an III) (12 March
1795).

she was well placed to succeed her in every sense; Langrand, at least, knew how to play the waiting game. The episode reveals another theme : that of loneliness. The country girl in Paris for the first time will be extremely grateful for company, and will be likely to take up with the first man who takes the trouble to talk to her and to take an interest in her. Langrand, who had been a *porteur d'eau*, would himself have been a provincial, almost certainly from the Aveyron. But, of course the important thing about this document is that Nicole and Langrand were living at the same address!

Marguerite Terrier, *tailleuse*, the daughter of a *chirurgien* from la Guillotière, met her seducer who was a student at the Ecole Royale Vétérinaire, which was also in this *commune*, just over the bridge from Lyon. It is much the same story with 'Dll. Antoinette Bally, dévideuse de soie à Lyon, y demeurant, maison de l'Oratoire, quai du Rhône, [qui] expose qu'elle a eu le malheur de faire la connaissance depuis plusieurs années du Sr. Pellorin fils … [qui] demeure chez son père, maître boulanger à la Guillotière'. It is easy enough to see how they must have met in the first place; the pont de la Guillotière was the physical link between them, an invitation in stone to bring them eventually together. Perhaps Pellorin met the girl on the Lyon side, quai du Rhône, on one of his visits to the city; or perhaps Antoinette had come across to la Guillotière on a week-end outing. What seems pretty certain is that the man's intentions were not serious; even though he had known the girl for several years, the son of a *maître boulanger* was unlikely to think of a *dévideuse* as a future wife. The chances are that he had been in the habit of crossing over, quai du Rhône, in the pursuit of pleasure.

Marie Dangle, *brodeuse*, had, we may remember, met her alleged seducer 'venant habituellement chez la soeur de la comparante où elle travaillait de son état de brodeuse'. Sisters are not always a protection, especially elder ones; they can be extremely dangerous. We will return later to the special case of Thérèse Bonnard, a woman undoubtedly *généreuse de sa personne*; but a *marchande fripière*, with her establishment in the rue Confort, would be likely to have a constant stream of visitors, as an old clothes shop would be almost as much in demand, at this level of society, as the *Mont de Piété* (which must also have been the point of departure of a great many romances, happy or unhappy, although it is never mentioned in the statements that we have used). Benoîte Bonnard met her man when she was 'demeurant rue Raisin, et près du domicile de Pierre Dusurgey, compagnon chapelier, ce voisinage donna lieu à ce dernier de faire connaissance avec elle; il lui faisait des visites fréquentes' (for he only had to cross the street). Marguerite Gulon, with an address 'à la Pierre Percée', would soon have come across

Dominique Bonhomme, who lived in the rue Saint-Georges. According to Bonhomme, he had first met the girl, who was a *brodeuse*, when he had brought her one of his waistcoats to be embroidered. Jeanne Rouzon, a year before her statement, had been apprenticed to a *tonnelier* of Caluire, and it was there that she had met François Bergeron, *garçon cordonnier*, who likewise lodged with his master. Bavet, *marchand drapier*, rue Saint-Nizier, was a neighbour of Françoise Dueure, *brodeuse*, who, when they first met, lived in the allée des Images, where 'il venait la voir assidument dans son domicile'. 'Dlle. Claudine Poncet, ouvrière demeurant chez Mlle. Royer, marchande de modes ... rue Mercière' stated 'que depuis environ une année et ½ la démontrante demeuroit dans la pension où logeoit le Sr. Antoine d'Audiffret', who had taken advantage of her youth—she was seventeen—to seduce her. Françoise Dubessy and Jean Biolay, as we have seen, had known each other in Pouilly-le-Monial; and the girl, on coming to Lyon, had sought him out : the usual story in fact of the lonely provincial girl in the big city. 'Catherine Marcel, fille domestique, demeurant à Lyon chez M. Dubour, place de la Charité ... a eu le malheur d'écouter les promesses séduisantes du Sr. François Bourdonneau, cuisinier chez M. Dubour.' Isabelle Collonge, *apprentie gazière*, apprenticed to a *gazier* of Cuire, states that she had been seduced by her master.

Antoinette Guillot, veuve Blanc, et Pierrette Blanc, sa fille, âgée de 20 ans ... dévideuse à Lyon, y demeurant rue Saint-Jean [déclarent] qu'au commence- ment de l'année dernière [1790] elles quittèrent Grézieu-la-Varenne, qu'elles avaient toujours habité, et vinrent se fixer en cette ville, elles prirent un logement dans la maison du Sr. Brigand, avocat, et elles passèrent bail pour 6 années. Le Sr. Brigand, profitant de sa qualité de locataire, en a abusé pour s'introduire dans le domicile des comparantes.

Clearly there was as much danger in being a tenant, as of taking up an abode in a lodging-house.

In most instances, the two would have met because they either lived in the same house, or were neighbours, or had met through work. Men obviously did not have to go very far to find a suitable companion. *On séduit de près plutôt que de loin*, or, to put it less grandly, one took the first opportunity that happened to turn up. So much for places, for the very obvious geography of 'where to meet'. Then there is the matter of timing, and this would obviously be dictated by week-ends, feast days, and public or private occasions. One of the witnesses for a *déclarante*, who was also her employee, after stating that 'la plaignante travaille chez elle, témoin, en qualité d'ouvrière depuis environ 6 années', was able to recall 'qu'elle a appris que la plaignante a fait la connaissance de P.D. le jour du mardi gras de l'année 1790'.

Anne Lassalle, brodeuse à Saint-Just, y demeurant chez son père, citoyen de Lyon, résidant Rue de Trion, paroisse de Saint-Just ... [déclare] qu'au mois d'octobre 1788 elle fut invitée pour assister à la cérémonie du baptême de l'enfant de Charlotte Grely, mariée à Jean-François Armanet, limonadier à la Guillotière, elle y fit connaissance de Louis Armanet, frère du père de l'enfant, elle était à peine âgée de 17 ans, Louis Armanet la combla de politesses et d'honnêtetés, abusant de son inexpérience, il la persuada que bientôt elle serait son épouse, il était âgé de 32 ans ... Quelques jours après, il lui fit chez son père une visite dans laquelle il lui exprima les mêmes sentimens, il continua et bientôt il lui tendit des pièges, il convenoit, suivant lui, d'avoir des entrevues particulières, il prétextoit la sévérité du père et de la mère de l'exposante ... la plaignante se rendoit dans les endroits qu'il lui indiquoit. Elle est devenue enceinte. Pendant sa grossesse il a montré tant d'empressement qu'elle ne pouvait le soupçonner de la tromper. Elle accoucha le 4 décembre 1790 d'une fille baptisée sous le nom de Marie, née d'elle et d'un père inconnu, elle a conservé son enfant, elle l'a allaitée et continue à l'allaiter dans la maison et sous les yeux de son père et de sa mère. Ils ont eu soin d'elle pendant sa grossesse. Il semble que le malheur qu'elle a éprouvé la leur a rendue plus chère ... Mais elle vient de s'apercevoir que son séducteur est un monstre . . . il a tenté de lui faire arracher son enfant, pour y parvenir, il a recours à différentes personnes. Le Sr. Pupier, l'un des frères de l'hôpital, est venu le lui demander en lui exposant que Louis Armanet avait payé entre les mains du recteur les droits d'entrée, il a fait l'impossible pour l'engager à le lui céder.

The only consoling, indeed unusual, feature in Anne's sad yet predictable narrative is the humanity and compassion displayed by her father and mother, both during her confinement and after the birth of Marie, an attitude that stands in marked contrast to those displayed, in similar circumstances, by most families (Dlle. Chirat: 'état qui l'a brouillée (avec assez de raison) avec sa famille, et principalement avec une tante'; Dlle. Faye: 'la comparante a été obligée de quitter sa famille pour venir cacher son malheur et sa honte en cette ville', and so on). The rest reads very much like a set piece. As the child was born in December, the fatal christening party must have taken place in March or April, at the beginning of spring, a season always favourable to enterprises of this kind. Armanet, who, we learn, was a blacksmith, was obviously an old hand at the game, but he had quite unusual advantages. For instance, having a brother who was a *limonadier* in la Guillotière would offer him at all times, but especially at week-ends and feast days during *la belle saison*, a particularly favourable terrain on which to operate, presumably as a single man, thanks to the presence, on such occasions, of large numbers of *brodeuses*, *dévideuses*, female domestics, and so on, coming either in parties of two—there might be some protection in this, but, more likely, two girls were better placed to play up a man or a couple of men—or in groups of four : two girls and two men —and most of these girls, making up for lost time in the sort of febrile pleasure that characterises the short hours of leisure of the very poor, would be likely to become very drunk in no time, thanks to the solicitude of the men friends whom they had brought with them or whom they had met at the *guinguette*. Then it might be a matter of retiring, there and then, into the conveniently enveloping shrubbery. But a *family* occasion, such as a christening, would offer even better opportunities, for it would cut down on the time devoted to the usual preliminary skirmishes—to the formalised *ballet d'amour* as stepped out, in a group of four, by two girls and two men : 'who are you?' 'you *would* like to know, wouldn't you?', 'can we have a guess?' and so on—as it would offer a perfect excuse for formal mutual introductions. The host would see to it that the two *brodeuses*, one of whom was possibly a friend of his wife's, should meet his brother, unattached and available—this would be pointed out by the *limonadier* or the hostess—who could then go right ahead, ply the girl with (free) drink and plenty of attention, charm her with his solicitude, tell her of his work and of his loneliness, prepare the ground for another meeting. Family affairs would always be the most dangerous. The only other aspect of Anne's story that seems somewhat atypical is the insistence of the blacksmith to have the child placed in a foundling hospital.

Spring and summer week-ends and feast days were certainly the most dangerous, apart from these family reunions. A witness, passing in the street, 'aux environs de la Saint-Jean dernier', recalls a couple glimpsed kissing and engaged in other *familiarités*. But February was likewise perilous, as can be illustrated from a case of rape, reported to the Minister of Justice, in March–April 1807, by the judicial authorities of Mons, at that time the *chef-lieu* of the Département de Jemappes :

> Un viol s'etant commis en la ville de Soignies ... ayant appris que 2 desd. prévenus avaient pris la fuite, et la rumeur publique m'ayant instruit qu'ils s'étaient enrôlés dans le régiment des Chevaux-légers Belges qui se formait à Liège, je me suis adressé à mon collègue en cette ville.[1]

And from a second letter we learn the following details :

> Il s'est commis un viol la nuit du 8 au 9 février dernier en la ville de Soignies sur une jeune fille honnête qui se trouvait dans une auberge où on donnait bal à cause du carnaval et qui est devenue la victime de la brutalité de plusieurs libertins. Il importe à la société que les coupables soient punis, un exemple devient d'autant plus nécessaire que déjà une jeune fille a été horriblement maltraité en la même ville.[2]

[1] *A.N.* BB 18 402 (Justice, Jemappes, directeur du jury d'accusation de Mons, au Grand Juge, le 7 avril 1807).
[2] *A.N.* BB 18 402 (Justice, Jemappes, directeur du jury d'accusation de Mons, au Grand Juge, le 11 mars 1807).

This is not, of course, to suggest that there existed an open or a closed season for the satisfaction of masculine lust, feminine desire, or mutual tenderness and affection expressed in the physical act of love. That would be nonsense, as the only seasonal variations would be those imposed by the monthly advent of what the French, rather unfairly, for we have not invaded that country all *that* frequently, describe as *les anglaises*. Otherwise, there would be no restrictions, apart from those imposed by space and opportunity : hence, as we have seen, the utility of a cellar, or a *maison de campagne*. What is revealed to us is only, of course, what, in one way or another, went wrong. The *déclarantes* are being forced out into the open by sheer need, coming forward, no doubt bashful and humiliated—so that many of them bring along with them workmates and employers, not just as witnesses, but for moral support—to be questioned by male judges, *greffiers*, or *commissaires de police* who generally show scant respect for their feelings, are not above giving them moral lectures on their conduct, and who often express scepticism as to their claims of innocence and inexperience.

Our material, it is perfectly clear, has no statistical value whatever; it is the product of chance, unlucky chance at that. *Le secret du boudoir, le langage de l'oreiller* do not obligingly speak to the enquiring social historian, and, perhaps in a majority of cases, we are dealing with an act between two people only and that takes place in intimacy, in a closed place, and in the absence of witnesses. Of such an act, it goes without saying, there is no written record, and even verbal recollection is generally to be discounted as solid evidence, owing to masculine habits of boastfulness. It is not the purpose of the historian to draw aside the curtains, and reveal *la Marquise* with her fine company of *quatre-vingts chasseurs*; we can leave that sort of thing to the old-fashioned *commissaire de police*, at a period when French divorce proceedings were less liberal and far more prying and indiscreet than at present. Nor are we attempting to render an act of mystery, tenderness and beauty a mere boon to the avid researcher, scrabbling for evidence. All this happened a very long time ago; and we are not insulting Pernon, Philippe, Victoire, and others, in thus revealing their ill-expressed secrets. Nor are we even particularly concerned, as they naturally would have been, with the physical consequences of the act itself, or with the name of the seducer. It is perhaps a little hard on these dead girls that we should seek profit from their terrible misfortunes and personal disasters; but, in this half-explored field of research, we have to clutch at any little hint that is going. We are searching for the fringe evidence, for the peripheral remarks that reveal, often quite unconsciously, generally accepted popular assumptions, the conventions of collective behaviour, *les politesses et les pudeurs* of the very poor and the very underprivileged, as much concerned with such externals as those at the top end of society (it might be noted, *en passant*, that the key word *l'honneur* recurs insistently in these documents, and that the honour of a *brodeuse* is potentially of greater value and of much more importance then that of a Duke, because it is all that she has got); public views as to what constitute a definitive commitment, made *au vu du monde* (and it is the fact of publicity that makes it so binding); the likeliest channels of movement within a city, the probable forms of the employment of leisure, the sociability and solidarity of the poor, even such physical matters as the number of people to a room, even to a bed, or where people meet. And it is for these reasons that we have placed so much emphasis on the collective, almost public aspects of what, in the end, would, in most cases, be the most private of all acts, though, in Lyon at least, it often seems to have commanded, *sauf votre respect*, a large, amused, and noisily appreciative audience.

The freedom of the street

What must stand out emphatically from much of this peripheral, almost incidental evidence that we have collected in support of the girls' statements (much of it a confused mumbling, a word spoken in parenthesis, a sudden slip of the tongue, or a heartfelt expression of prejudice, or the warming appeal of solidarity), at least to anyone not conversant with the tiny compensations of life as it presented itself to the working population and the lower orders in an eighteenth-century city, is the relative freedom of movement, outside, in the street, from street to street, enjoyed by all those with whom we have been concerned. The *brodeuse*, the *dévideuse*, the *coupeuse*, the *tailleuse*, the *blanchisseuse*, the *apprêteuse*, the *marchande de modes*, even the domestic servant, like their various masculine equivalents, are constantly walking the city, especially within the central peninsular, and bearing the handy and visible pretext of some errand[1]—a half-finished waistcoat, a three-cornered hat awaiting its trimmings and plumes, a dress that still needs to be embroidered, a woman's hat that has still to be ironed into shape, a basket of wet linen, a bouquet containing a note, a dozen bottles of wine, a tray containing a meal prepared by a *gargotier*, a tray containing

[1] The wisdom in thus carrying, as visibly as possible, the external symbols of a legitimate occupation, at all times, was not confined to eighteenth-century France. When I was employed as a sanitary orderly, in the British Army, at one stage of the Second World War, emptying lavatories and cleaning out urinals on Chepstow Race Course, it was impressed upon me most succinctly, by a Welsh corporal, my colleague and mentor: 'Always have a hard brush and pail to hand, bach, in case the sarge comes by; he won't come *too* close, owing to the stink. Believe me, bach, you are in a safe billet in a job like this which makes you stink. They won't interfere with you.' And they didn't. But I always had the pail and hard brush to hand.

cakes and pastries, a brace of pheasants, a box of tools, a sack full of old clothes—the tell-tale passports to the freedom of outside during working hours. Mobility within the city, the pretext to wander the streets in daytime, the freedom of movement of the female artisan, servant and shopgirl were the minor, but appreciable privileges enjoyed by the hard-worked and the exploited, and that often distinguished them from girls of superior social status and economic resources whose valuable virtue could not thus be exposed to the manifold hazards of the street-corner and the doorstep conversation and encounter. Restif and Mercier were quick to point out that, in this respect, *la fille de l'artisan, l'ouvrière, la grisette*, even *la fille de salle*, enjoyed a measure of freedom, often within the whole length and breadth of Paris, that would have been totally denied to *la fille du marchand*, and the girl of high condition. It was perhaps a minor compensation for terribly long working hours, frightful working conditions, and overcrowded lodgings, bad food, and only occasional drink, and that of poor quality. But it offered in return a wealth of gossip, information, sociability, amusement, contact, friendship and humour. The 'freedom of the street' was not to be disdained merely as a few moments gained, surreptitiously, from the monotony and extreme fatigue of the working day.

For one thing, many of these female trades were by nature peripatetic. The marvellous mobility of the *blanchisseuse* has often been remarked upon, both by contemporaries and by historians; and because she com-manded her small continents of streets, quays and bridges, because she spent much of her time walking from quarter to quarter, and because she possessed, in her basket, the passport to the interior, albeit to the servants' quarters, of the houses of the great, her services were also much in demand with those who were criminally inclined. It is perhaps less often realised that even a silk worker will spend much of her working hours outside the workshop or the shop, taking samples, picking up materials, taking hats to be finished; for at this level of *l'artisanat*, pro-duction would not be confined to a single workshop, to the room of a single *maître-tailleuse*, there will be a whole range of finishers, *apprêteurs* and *apprêteuses, fourbisseurs* and *fourbisseuses*, so that the completed article would be likely to have passed through half-a-dozen different hands, and to have travelled, on an apparently meaningless course, doubling back on its tracks, climbing *montées*, even crossing one of the rivers, half across the city, before at last reaching the shop of the *marchande de modes*; and even that will not be its final destination; for the servant of the eventual purchaser, who was possibly also the *commanditaire*, would be sent to pick it up and bring it back to a grimly shuttered, fortress-like *hôtel particulier* in Ainay or Perrache, its prison-like walls blind to the excitements and activities of the streets.

The *soyeurs* and the *bons bourgeois de Lyon* must have paid heavily for their constant search for privacy and security in a great deal of boredom; *ennui* has never been an ailment of the common people.

This would apply particularly to a luxury industry like silk, almost every article of which would have been made to order and according to very strict specifications. The *commanditaire* would thus want to see the progress of the article at each stage, and, in the case of clothing of any kind, there would be a whole series of fittings, each of which would be an occasion for one of the junior *apprenties brodeuses* or *fileuses* to cross the quarter, or several quarters, carrying the dress, the coat, the hat, or the skirt. As these hand-made articles were of considerable and lasting value, they would have to be handled with great care, protected from the elements, especially from rain or snow, or from the glare of the summer sun. So the elements too could be allies of a walking girl's outside leisure : a pause in a covered entry during a shower, a pause in the shade of a *traboule* so as to protect the bright colours from the midday sun; and each pause would be put to profit in the form of conversation. In Paris, during the revolutionary period, Fouquier-Tinville and his like received a great deal of valuable information from working and walking women—as well as from stationary ones like portresses and *concierges*—who knew how to use their eyes and ears, and who could report on anything unusual, anything out of place, whether a gathering on the Pont-Neuf, or a bigger crowd than customary at the *café Chrétien*. Much of the immense body of papers of the former Public Prosecutor consists of information derived from this type of observant source. So in Lyon, at a later stage of the revolutionary period, the semi-secret armies of the White Terror were in receipt of copious, often hour by hour information regarding the *faits et gestes* of members of the garrison, hated strangers in the city, the object of uniform opprobrium, who could not even set foot beyond the safety of the barracks, in pairs, or in larger groups, without being designated, in advance, as they walked down from la Croix-Rousse or crossed over from la Guillotière, by female scouts, standing in doorways or apparently going about their normal business, by prostitutes, on their usual beats, by girls looking out of upper windows. The social solidarity of a city population engaged largely in a single trade would now be further reinforced by an even stronger bond of *political* solidarity, taking the form of bitter hostility to Paris, a carefully nurtured sense of local grievance, and feeding on the terrible memories of the Siege and the *mitraillades*.

Mobility within the city—one would be tempted to call it the freedom of the city within working hours; the easy, friendly and mocking sociability of the street, of the open-doored wine-shop, *échoppe*, *gargote*, shoemaker's shop, indeed, of all those artisans and tradesmen who lived

open-doored on to the street, as if not to miss anything of the passing
theatre; the bustle, noise and gossip of the main markets—the *salons* of
the poor, the parlour of *la Mère Duchesne* and her kind (but, in Lyon,
la Mère Duchesne would entertain very different political views from
those stridently stated by her *cousine* in Paris); the brief respite offered
by *la Promenade* and by the quays, the availability of the network of
the *traboules*, which, as well as furnishing ready escape routes to the
swift-footed malefactor or political assassin, offered a convenient cover-
ing, a brief extra tunnel of illicit leisure, to the dawdling apprentice,
the whistling child *commissionnaire*, or the pretty *tailleuse*, happily
aware of the attention of which she was the moving object—all constituted one of the principal compensations for those obliged to spend long
hours indoors, in dark and airless cellars or ground-floor rooms, using
up their eyesight on minute embroidery or on complicated stitching, in a
city in which most houses would have as many as seven storeys. It is as
if the many errands that could legitimately be fitted into working hours,
discreetly prolonged, even repeated—it was so easy to forget some small
object, a thimble might be the excuse to return over three streets—
formed the preparation for the much greater, exhilarating, almost
limitless freedom of the week-end, when joyful little bands of workmates,
two girls, two men, headed for *la Promenade* or *le champ de la
Fédération.* One can picture the *brodeuse*, as, on her way, she takes in
a small, shaded square, a cool fountain, a wine-shop, its entry covered
with a trellis of roses or cool ivy, or a handsome butcher's apprentice,
standing proudly in his bloody apron, and makes mental notes to return
there longer, to investigate here further, on the longed-for free afternoon,
or in the coolness of a summer evening. For the life of the urban poor is
probably at its worst indoors, where it would be subjected to constant
scrutiny on the part of the *marchande de modes* or of the *tailleuse.* The
view from within was a window on to freedom, the promise of adventure.
How often, in our statements, do we encounter such phrases : 'que le 15
ou 16 juin dernier, allant porter une paire de souliers à François Baroud,
il entra dans la boutique' (this of a *compagnon cordonnier*); 'elle a eu la
visite du Sr. V., maître tailleur . . . sous prétexte d'acheter des marchandises' (this of a *marchande fripière*, whose adventures will concern
us shortly); 'ajoute que ladite Bonnard vient habituellement chercher du
pain chez lui' (this of a *maître boulanger*, and, as Henri Béraud reminds
us, in his marvellous *La Gerbe d'Or*, the *boulangerie-pâtisserie* is the
people's forum for the whole of les Terreaux, receiving as it does the more
leisurely Sunday trade as well as that of the week with less time to waste
in talk); 'elle . . . est allée plusieurs fois chez la plaignante . . . pour lui
rendre du linge' (this of a *blanchisseuse*). Jeanne Caillot, *brodeuse*, states :
'il y a nombre d'années que le commerce de broderies a amené dans son

domicile le Sr.... commis chez le Sr.... marchand brodeur' (for *brodeuses* generally worked in the house in which they slept : the seventh floor for much-needed sleep, the ground-floor for the long hours of work, so that it was an easy ascent from the latter to the former for the man who made regular visits to the workshop).

What emerges from these snippets of information is that the companions of leisure had often been recruited, in the course of the working week, in the *camaraderie* of the street, in the hoped-for hazards of errands. 'Can I come and fetch you on Sunday?' 'Shall we all go to *la Promenade* together at the week-end?' And this will end us up with some statement such as this : 'Marguerite Pagot, coupeuse de poils à Lyon, y demeurant, rue Raisin, âgée de 24 ans... [déclare] qu'elle a habité avec la plaignante, avec laquelle elle couchait chez la veuve Anciau ... qu'elle ... a même été souvent de leur promenade', while another witness, Jean-Baptiste Brossard, *cordonnier*, living rue du Cornet, and aged twenty-three, also adds the information 'qu'il s'est souvent promené avec eux'—a foursome of twenty-three- and twenty-four-year-olds, resulting in the pregnancy of one of the girls. In other words, leisure could be more dangerous than work, because it carried a relationship begun during working-hours a stage further, bearing the girl, as on an invisible stream, that much nearer to the perils of seduction. And, ultimately, there is perhaps no great safety in numbers, save to provide the ill-used girl with ready witnesses in her hour of need. Even so, at least at the tentative stage of the relationship, the couple chooses to be accompanied by another couple, even by two more couples. Six can make more noise and have more boisterous fun than four, *on partage*, so that the money will go further, and, with a reserve of two other men to dance with, or to flirt with, the girl has an extra hold over the young man who is attempting to make the running.

Of course, as far as women and girls are concerned, this freedom of movement should not be exaggerated, especially in revolutionary terms. The Revolution gave *men* a greater passport to the freedom of the road, as well as to the freedom of the night. (We will hear of a man who states 'lorsqu'il venait passer la nuit avec la plaignante, il faisait entendre à sa femme qu'il allait passer la nuit au piquet de garde'; but a woman had no guard duties, and the National Guard would thus offer her no alibi.) Women, especially in the silk industry, could cadge the odd half-hour of freedom here and there, in the course of the day, but their mobility would hardly extend beyond the bounds of the city. *Le retour au pays* would be the worst, because the most humiliating, of all solutions, while pregnancy, above all, will severely restrict the possibilities of escape from an urban environment and from the relentless search for alternative employment following dismissal. It is the male who holds all the cards in this respect; if the worst comes to the worst, he can always opt out altogether by volunteering. And he will not be ill thought of, save by the girl whom he has abandoned.

The days and the nights of the rue Confort

On 14 January 1791, Dlle. Thérèse Bonnard, giving her profession as *marchande fripière*, rue Confort, came before the judge. In her statement, she said that seven months previously 'elle a eu la visite du Sr. Vermillière, maître-tailleur, rue Bourgchanin, sous prétexte d'acheter des marchandises, il est resté longtems, est revenu, disant qu'il était libre tandis qu'il était marié... [il] lui a fait des promesses de mariage'. Giving her age as twenty-six, she added that she was now six months pregnant.

The judge was not impressed, for he had taken the trouble to inform himself from other, and as it turned out, numerous and loquacious sources. Dlle Bonnard's ground-floor abode facing on to the rue Confort might have been described as 'a room with a view', but one that looked inwards, rather than outwards; and a majority of the inhabitants of her street, as well as plenty of passers-by, by day or in the middle of the night—for, during the previous summer, plenty of them seem to have been still up and about well after midnight—had taken to looking inward, while almost as many had indeed 'looked in'. Yet it is clear from the numerous witnesses heard by the judge that the girl, though apparently extremely accommodating to a succession of male visitors, was not popular, either with those who had enjoyed her favours or with the other inhabitants of the street and the quarter. But a popular *marchande fripière* would be something of a phenomenon in eighteenth-century conditions; for hers was an occupation that preyed on poverty, debt and improvidence. The *fripière* was the pawn-broker of those in desperate straits for the next meal. It was the last resort : after pots and pans and cooking utensils, would come clothes, first those that were not immediately needed by the requirements of the season, then pretty well the whole wardrobe, save what actually covered one's nakedness.

The first witness to be heard is François Prime, *fabricant de bas*, aged thirty-five, living rue Bourgchanin, who

dépose que Thérèse Bonnard est connue dans tout le canton pour une fille de mauvaise vie, que lui témoin ayant été appellé plusieurs fois par lad. Bonnard, a eu la faiblesse d'avoir des habitudes avec elle, que chaque fois qu'il est allé la voir, il lui en a coûté son argent, qu'elle fit confidence au témoin il y a environ 3 mois et ½ qu'elle étoit enceinte des oeuvres du nommé Ragoût, marchand, toilier, qu'il a su qu'elle couchoit habituellement pendant l'automne dernier avec un Sr. Rambaud, chirurgien ... que lui a cessé d'aller chez elle, parce qu'il craignoit qu'elle ne lui mît le paquet sur le corps.

So much for the not very gallant Prime. Then there is the picturesque Jean Fleury Font, who, as well as describing himself as 'tambour du canton de [la] rue Bellecordière et de la place Neuve', aged thirty-eight, is something of a humourist out of *Guignol's* répertoire :

... dépose que la fille Bonnard lui a fait confidence d'avoir eu des habitudes avec un marchand de violons, et avec un nommé Ragoût, marchand toilier, qu'elle était fiancée avec le marchand de violons, que c'étoient 2 drôles qui cherchoient à lui jouer des tours orduriers en plaçant à sa porte mille choses indécentes, accompagnées de lettres remplies d'infamies, qu'ils l'avaient mise dans la peine, mais qu'elle préférait garder ce qu'elle avait et ne les plus revoir, qu'elle proposa à lui témoin de surveiller led. Ragoût et le marchand de violons pour les surprendre lorsqu'ils viendroient déposer à la porte de lad. Bonnard les objets indécens dont elle se plaignait, que lui témoin a en con- séquence fait le guet avec un nommé Gilet, tambour du Plâtre, pendant 2 nuits après le piquet [de la garde] retiré, que la 3me nuit entre minuit et une heure il rencontra lad. Bonnard, assise avec le nommé Ragoût sur le Quai Monsieur, qu'étonné lui témoin dit à la fille Bonnard, *il ne valait pas la peine de nous faire passer deux nuits pour arrêter des personnes avec qui vous êtes si bien d'accord*, que lad. Bonnard s'en fut avec led. Ragoût, que depuis ce moment il ne lui a pas parlé.

The next in line is Augustin Rimbaud, *chirurgien*, 'greffier de la municipalité de Saint-Martin-la-Plaine, y demeurant ... 32 ans', who states

qu'il a travaillé en qualité de clerc chez le Sr. Achard, chirurgien en cette ville, place Grenouille,[1] que la tante de Thérèse Bonnard, demeurante porte à porte avec le Sr. Achard, lui témoin y fit la connaissance de lad. Bonnard avec laquelle il eut des habitudes dès les premiers instants, ce qui lui donna fort mauvaise idée de la vertu de cette fille ... dans le courant de l'été dernier, étant allé demeurer chez le Sr. Pointe, chirurgien en cette ville ... il eut occasion de passer sous les fenêtres de lad. Bonnard ... que cette fille l'appella et l'engagea à la visiter pour savoir si elle était enceinte, que lui témoin confirma lad. Bonnard dans ses soupçons ... depuis son séjour chez led. Sr. Pointe, il a joui encore à plusieurs reprises de lad. Bonnard ... qu'elle vouloit que le témoin lui administrât des remèdes pour la faire avorter, mais qu'il s'y est refusé.

Rimbaud seems to have had a little professional conscience, but not much else. Although in the medical profession, and knowing the risks, he continues to enjoy the perilous favours of la Bonnard while at the same time, blackening her morally. The next witness is a woman, Marie Chise,

[1] On Jacques-Joseph Achard, born in Lyon, parish of Saint-Nizier, 29 May 1765, see Dr Jean Rousset, 'Un chirurgien Jacobin: "L'Infernal Achard" ' (*Albums du Crocodile*, No. 1, Lyon, 1964).

femme d'antoine Duplan, blanchisseuse à Lyon, y demeurant, rue Ferrandière, âgée de 62 ans ... qu'étant plusieurs fois chez la plaignante et notamment dans le commencement de ce mois pour lui rendre du linge ... elle y a vu ... le Sr. Vermillière ... cette dernière racontait au Sr. Vermillière que sa femme étoit venue chez elle lui faire des reproches de ce qu'elle voyoit son mari, à quoi led. Vermillière répondit qu'il étoit fâché de donner du chagrin à sa femme, qu'il ne croyoit pas qu'elle eût pu découvrir leur liaison, parce que lorsqu'il venait passer la nuit avec la plaignante, il faisait entendre à sa femme qu'il alloit passer la nuit au piquet de garde, cherchant led. Vermillière à consoler la plaignante en lui promettant quelques écus de tems en tems.

François Thévenon merely states 'qu'il étoit voisin de la demeure de la plaignante, il a vu un particulier vêtu de gris frapper sur le contrevent de la fenêtre de la plaignante, qui habite au rez-de-chaussée.' The last witness is Réne Cordonnier, *portefaix*, who states

seulement que passant dans le courant du mois d'août dernier entre 10 heures et 11 heures du soir au-devant de la boutique de la plaignante ... il vit le Sr. Vermillière qui frappait avec son chapeau contre la fenêtre de la plaig- nante, qu'il se suspendit même à lad. fenêtre qui est au rez-de-chaussée, que lad. Bonnard ouvrit sa fenêtre et appella ce particulier par son nom, qu'elle vint ensuite lui ouvrir la porte de l'allée et il entra.

Unfortunately, that is all that we know about Thérèse Bonnard and her matrimonial affairs. Clearly, in view of her trade, she was likely to have had some money of her own, and Vermillière, although married, as a *maître tailleur*, would have been a better proposition for her than a *marchand toilier*, a *marchand de violons*, or even a *chirurgien*. Nor is one concerned to decide whether the girl, so much abused by the testi- mony of men who made no difficulty about admitting that they had enjoyed her favours, not merely once, but on a number of occasions, with or without payment, deserved the reputation that she had obviously acquired with many of her neighbours of both sexes and of different ages, and with the inhabitants as a whole of the *canton* of the rue de la Bellecordière. The rue Confort is a microcosm of life, at all hours by day and by night, *entre Rhône-et-Saône*, very near the quays of both rivers, but nearer to the Saône. On a hot August night a *tambour* en- counters the so-called lovers, quai Monsieur; and, on other summer nights, there are plenty of witnesses, even after midnight, to the muted life of the narrow street; living on the ground floor, Dlle. Bonnard might as well have been living on a stage, her every movement and gesture watched by sleepless or merely inquisitive neighbours, one of whom can hear her call Vermillière by name as he attempts to climb up to window level. After the night watch has passed, there seem still to be plenty of people in the street, and they are certainly not minding their own business; some, on their own admission, take the opportunity to place unpleasant

objects—either excrement or primitive contraceptives—as well as insulting notes and messages, at the girl's door. Those who observe her and
those who enjoy her favours belong to the whole range of the local
population of the *canton,* from *portefaix* and *blanchisseuses,* to master-
craftsmen, shopkeepers, merchants, doctors and apprentices. Her case is a
dramatic, and therefore perhaps somewhat untypical example of the
sociability of a collectivity that is still perpendicular rather than hori-
zontal, a unit in which the passer-by will look upwards, rather than to
the front. And although all these people would have had a very hard
day's work, many seem still to have had the energy and the inclination
to fool about at night, whether to tap at Thérèse's window, or to watch
at her door. The two *tambours,* for instance, were eager to accept her
challenge, though they had no particular reason to act on her behalf;
but she was fooling *them.* At least this is what Font must have thought
when he met her with her lover (her alleged persecutor) on the quay, well
after midnight, on his third successive night keeping watch. Restif seems
to have had plenty of imitators in this almost southern city, in which, in
August at least, there would have been much more to satisfy their impudent curiosity than in Paris.

Conclusion

We have been engaged on an excursion into the hidden life and assumptions of a pre-industrial society, the principal characteristic of which is
perhaps the very shadowy frontier between work and leisure. It is a
pattern of life that is not governed by the stop-watch or the factory
whistle, and which, owing to the many successive stages that brings a
piece of raw material to the final, completed article, allows the artisan
a certain freedom of movement, limited perhaps in time, none the less
difficult fully to control or to check. The picture that emerges, though
one of extremely long working hours, in unhealthy conditions, and
dominated, in the case of women, by the constant fear of summary dismissal, as a result of pregnancy, is not one of an existence entirely heartless, devoid of compassion, enjoyment, fun, and rowdy pleasure. There
are the compensations of companionship, mutual help, and the gusty
enjoyments of the very poor, of those who are prepared to make a little
go a long way, of those who will eagerly pick up anything that is going
for nothing, from a piece of fruit lying in the street, to a cool breeze
over the Rhône, from the music of a street band of *Savoyards,* with their
dancing bear and their monkey, from the hard-hitting puppets of
Guignol, to the massed choirs of *la fête de la Fédération,* from the pomp,
awe, excitement, majesty and naïveté of a religious procession, to the
pleasure of sitting in the sun, with a male friend, on the quays, from the

quite exceptional, rumbustious, and dangerous excitement of a christening or a wedding, to the calmer pattern of a Sunday spent at home, over an unambitious *ragoût*, followed by a stroll, from the enjoyment of a street dispute, to a brief conversation with a young man standing outside a shop. There is in fact a considerable range of wealth and experience in these unsophisticated and often unexpected enjoyments, and one can, from the material that we have employed, appreciate the gusto and vigour with which the common people threw themselves into leisure, despite, or perhaps because of, the very precariousness and discomfort of their daily existence. Gwynne Lewis has elsewhere remarked upon this apparent disparity between wretchedness and rumbustiousness,[1] and it has been our intention to illustrate it further and in depth, even to suggest that, far from there being a contradiction between the realities of life and the breezy optimism so often displayed towards them, the one produced the other. One does not have the impression that this was a society that was sad or sick. It was certainly very uncomfortable; but it could also rise to simple, even ecstatic joy, and to a completely uninhibited enjoyment of the passing moment, without a thought for what would follow. What would follow, of course, was the early rise in the morning, and the prospect of another long working day. But even that would not be entirely predictable, it would contain elements of uncertainty, the possibility of a chance encounter, the promise of a brief escape into the swirling freedom of the open street. Indeed, *nothing* would ever be entirely predictable, save that, inexorable, of the advance of a pregnancy. And even that might not be the unmitigated disaster it would appear to have been at first sight : a number of these girls seem to have been eager to keep their children, a few of them were fortunate enough to have had parents who were understanding and helpful.[2]

We have also sought, by exploring behind the formal words of standard legal phraseology, to penetrate a language rich in hidden assumptions, and hinting at the elements of a popular collective morality, of an alternative system of justice, even of a popular religiosity, all of which were

[1] Gwynne Lewis, *Life in Revolutionary France* (London, 1971), p. 112: 'Yet, when one has tabulated the misery provoked by a fairly heartless society, produced graphs to show the high incidence of suicide in 1796 or deaths from cholera and typhus during the last years of the Empire, one is still confronted with a residual enjoyment of life among the *classes populaires* which appears, at first glance, inexplicable. There were times, however, when "joy was unconfined"; for example, the Sunday visits to the small, crowded inns on the outskirts of Paris ...'

[2] It is interesting, for instance, to note, that of the fifty-odd *déclarations* that we have used, only one, that of Thérèse Bonnard, mentions the possibility of an abortion. According to one of the young *chirurgiens* quoted, she had called down from her window, asking him if he could conduct one for her himself. She did not even make any secret of her intentions, shouted out to the young man as he went by, *en pleine rue.*

parallel to, and not necessarily hostile to, official morality, official religion, and the carefully defined rights and wrongs of the new Codes. In this sense, our task has been in the nature of an *explication de textes*, of a close examination of the wording of our *déclarations*, not so much in an effort to put a name to the seducer—a matter of indifference to the historian—as to pick up the hints. Thus, we have been concerned primarily with a study of language; and language and history are so closely tied that even translation is likely, by forcing the former through an artificial and diluting filter, to dull the full impact of meaning and emphasis, tone and half-tone, vigour and reticence (not that we can find very much reticence either in the *milieu* we have been examining, or in the language in which it is expressed). Even so it is not the direct language of the girl, as she poured out her woes to the judge or the *commissaire*, in that unmistakable, rather slow, rather hesitant speech, as if feeling its way, careful to avoid a southern gabble of words, or the cheeky impudence of the Parisian accent, apparently rather lazy, as if the speaker were only half awake, in fact very careful, always with the listener in mind, always ready to beat an instant retreat in the face of the slightest sign, even a visible one, of offence or objection : in short, *l'accent lyonnais*, a manner of speech and a tone of voice unique, like everything about that city, indicative itself of a careful, prudent, watchful vigilance, even perhaps of a fundamental pessimism, though thoughtless optimism seems to have been what guided the leisure of most of the *déclarantes*. To reconstruct their speech and their accent requires an effort of imagination, though not an insuperable one, as one attempts to hear through the muffling blanket set upon the girls' voices by the formality and toneless monotony of legal language. If, at times, we have succeeded at least in this : in allowing the girls to explain themselves in their own simple, often tragic, words, then we have indeed achieved what we set out to do : to view, from the level of these *brodeuses* and *dévideuses, la vie lyonnaise* of the early 1790s—the date would have had little meaning for people in their condition, though it might reach down to them through the fluctuations and eventual slump in the silk trade and manufacture—the predictable pattern of the day, the equally predictable and grim prospect of the immediate future, at the stage at which we leave them, to their uncertain, often dangerous fate, just this side of conception, and before the advent of a further generation of witnesses to the continuity of that life, witnesses born, so often as an indirect result of *la Promenade*, in the early 1790s, most of whom would thus be likely to experience the very different quality of life and public events in the Lyon of the 1830s.

INDEX OF PLACES